INTRODUCTION

Leaving America: Not Easy

Hurrah! That US Army shout describes how I used to feel about America.

Hurrah! That's how I feel about Russia now.

It is easy to condemn America these days. The country has changed so much that many in and out of my generation can't accept what it has become. We were raised by family and community to believe that America stood for what is right and good in the world. But somewhere along the American way, we lost that right and good and it seems likely the loss is permanent.

The United States has always had issues throughout its history. We've made many mistakes. Yet we always seemed to be able to make corrections to get back on the right course. There was a sense of humility that accompanied acknowledgement of the errors of the past, even those connected to the present.

For me America the change started with the Vietnam War with which I am intimately familiar: I was drafted into the US Army and was shipped off to fight in that war.

I noticed some of the changes like everyone else in the country did during the later stages of that war. The disillusionment that we felt from getting whipped by the Vietcong and North Vietnamese wounded the American psyche. But even with that tragic mistake the country healed itself and moved along its historical path, apparently back to greatness, until it encountered a crossroads of sorts. At that crossroad was a path to the 'right thing to do' and roads to complacency, greed,

INTRODUCTION

corruption, identity politics and hubris. It seems that doing the right thing was too hard for America and so we all seemed to rush to turn to those paths that have put the United States where it is today: At war, polarized, greedy and dangerous to itself and the world.

I have fond memories of the America I used to know. I could ramble on about its potential and how most Americans reveled in its dominance and sincerely thought the nation a force for good in the world. We really did try to do what was correct and moral based on Church teachings of the day. But now I fear that Americans have lost God and the willingness to sacrifice and fight the good fight.

Volunteer Army: Death Wish for Others

I was drafted into the US Army. I was drafted to go and kill and maim other human beings around the world. I strongly support a draft. Why? Many I knew during the Vietnam War years were reluctant to go and kill other human beings but did it to survive and come home. Now, though, the US military is made up of volunteers who have a desire, a wish to kill. Most of us who were drafted to fight in Vietnam did not have a death wish for other human beings. That, in my mind, has become a moral issue. The worst living nightmare we had in those years was the young Americans begging to join the US Army and claiming, "I want to kill the Gooks". Turns out they were usually the first ones killed in combat." I would say to me fellow soldiers, "It's just weeding out the riff-raff."

From my perspective, political correctness and identity politics have had a chilling effect on American society. In my time, calling a girl a girl was fine. For those of you thinking I'm

INTRODUCTION

intolerant, I'd like you to know my father was a gay man. He fought in the Korean War. He was a leader in high school education and a coach. He raised me to have a strong moral compass, and, yes, to call a girl a girl. His view on being gay was this: It does not matter who I love or why. What matters is if I flaunt my lifestyle in other people's faces.

I remember silver and gold certificates: Real money! Not just a piece of paper that claimed to have worth. I recall Blue Laws enforced around the nation on Sunday's which used to be viewed as a sacred day of rest. Shopping centers and other businesses were closed so that employees could be with family and friends and rest in accordance with the 7th Day. That day was also a time of reflection, to think about sacrifice and freedom.

I remember a time when the police would catch us drunk and silly but instead of zip cuffs on the wrists, they would call the parents or drive us home. The police did not shoot first and ask questions later. But with so many weapons on the streets and in the home, that has changed. I grew up and felt pride in our police who patrolled our small town. It seemed that any issue could be resolved without resorting to a gun.

America had a chance to show the world that we were, as we say, "Number One" and hold that ranking through the strength of compassion, humility and unimpeachable moral barometers. That is the country I love, with all my heart. The fact is, the United States can still work its way back into the light and demonstrate to the world that it can fulfill its potential.

INTRODUCTION

Someone my age remembers when the AT&T-Bell System controlled all the telecommunications networks in the United States. It was, of course, a monopoly. The United States Department of Justice Antitrust Division broke up that monopoly. To what end? I look around and see nothing but monopolies bigger that the AT&T-Bell System ever was. Government intervention back then, in my view, has led to a situation in which the American government is used as a tool of big monopolies. The American people have no voice in these matters.

I Left for Russia but I Still Love America

I drifted to Russia and found what I needed to cure my heartache and dismay at what America had lost. Russia is far from perfect, but for me it is a country in which people still can act like people without having to wear awkward social masks. It is also a place, unlike depicted in the Western media, where people have few fears of government intervention in their lives. But that does not mean I do not love America. I see hope there and that hope is rooted in the American people.

I am saddened by what has happened to America. Saddened that many people cannot see what has happened and saddened by the fact that people will defend the policies and morals that now define the nation. I want to love America, but sometimes we must let those go who we love the most. The United States has become that terrible family uncle that everyone tries to love—but in spite of that love, he keeps doing things that hurts the family.

Kyle Keeton is a United States Army veteran of the Vietnam War. He runs the website Windows to Russia. Kyle lives in a small village in rural Russia

DEDICATION
Damien, Jill, Scylla, Neisha, Peanut, JC, AG, D+L, LFS, K, MB

CONTENTS

CONTENTS

Modern Day America: 100 Years from the Third Reich?

October 31, 2014: *"Unbeknownst to most Americans the United States is presently under thirty presidential declared states of emergency. They confer vast powers on the Executive Branch including the ability to financially incapacitate any person or organization in the United States, seize control of the nation's communications infrastructure, mobilize military forces, expand the permissible size of the military without congressional authorization, and extend tours of duty without consent from service personnel. Declared states of emergency may also activate Presidential Emergency Action Documents and other continuity-of-government procedures which confer powers on the President, such as the unilateral suspension of habeas corpus—that appear fundamentally opposed to the American constitutional order. Although the National Emergencies Act, by its plain language, requires the Congress to vote every six months on whether a declared national emergency should continue, Congress has done only once in the nearly forty year's history of the Act."* **Patrick Thronson, Michigan Journal of Law (2013, Vol 46).**

A bit of irony, perhaps, that on November 4, 2014—as Americans go to the polls to cast their ballots for a slate of politicians at the local, state and federal levels—the august citizens of the United States will also celebrate the birth of the National Security Agency (NSA).

On November 4, 1952, the NSA was created by a Presidential Executive Order signed by then president Harry Truman. Earlier that year, in January 1952, Truman's state of the union address focused on the Korean War, the global Soviet-Communist threat, the "Iran oil situation", and the need to increase the production of US military equipment for use by American forces, and for transfer to Western European Allies. Truman called on Americans to seek guidance in the God of Peace even as a brutal shadow war was being waged by the United States to eliminate popularly elected "leftist" governments.

In 1953 Dwight D. Eisenhower was elected to the American presidency and with him came John Foster and Allan Dulles, two political appointees who would, it turns out, seek the counsel and expertise of "former" Nazi executioners, scientists and intelligence operatives. J Edgar Hoover, then director of the Federal Bureau of Investigation (FBI), was already on the case using whatever resources were at his disposal—including Nazis–to hunt down unionists, communists, dissenters and radicals wherever they might be. According to the UK's Guardian newspaper, Truman had this to say about Hoover and his FBI, "We want no Gestapo or secret police. FBI is tending in that direction. They are dabbling in sex-life scandals and plain blackmail... Edgar Hoover would give his right eye to take over, and all congressmen and senators are afraid of him."

From 1953-1961, Eisenhower, as Commander in Chief, constructed a nascent military-intelligence-law enforcement-industrial complex influenced directly by Nazi ideology and technological know-how. No wonder he warned the world about his creation, the military-industrial complex. At one time in the early 21st Century it was uncomfortable to call out America's ties to the Nazis. But that has changed particularly with the release of Eric Lichtblau's The Nazis Next Door (2014) and The Collaboration by Ben Urwand. It has also been confirmed by the overthrow of a nationally elected leader in Ukraine—Victor Yanukovych–and the open support of neo-Nazi groups largely responsible for that event. Is it a coincidence that the head of the CIA, John Brennan, visited with the neo-Nazi usurpers not long after the coup given the CIA's history?

Do You Want to Know a Secret, do, da, do?

According to Lichtblau, writing in the New York Times, *"The full tally of Nazis-turned-spies is probably much higher', said Norman Goda, a University of Florida historian...but many records remain classified even today, making a complete count impossible. U.S. agencies directly or indirectly hired numerous ex-Nazi police officials and East European collaborators who were manifestly guilty of war crimes, he said. Information was readily available that these were compromised men. The wide use of Nazi spies grew out of a Cold War mentality shared by two titans of intelligence in the 1950s: Mr. Hoover, the longtime F.B.I. director, and Mr. Dulles, the C.I.A. director."*

Over at Antiwar.com, in "Federal Agencies Just Doing Whatever They Want Now" Lucy Steigerwald comments wryly on Lichtblau's findings: *"...the CIA hid their precious assets from Nazi hunters and prosecutors trying to deport then-old men in the 1980s and even into the '90s. Most disturbing, one of Holocaust architect Adolf Eichmann's little buddies, Otto von Bolschwing, was protected until 1982, when he conveniently died of a brain disorder before he could be deported or prosecuted. Famously, Nazi rocket scientists were picked up by America to prevent their expertise from falling into Soviet hands. Maybe an exception to the prickly feeling that letting heinous war criminals off the hook is not what America was supposed to be doing when it won the good war in a heroically-sepia montage could be made for geniuses like Wernher Von Braun. Von Braun was a rocket scientist and "honorary" SS member under the Nazis, and he helped*

America get to the moon (which is neat, so that apparently makes his debated level of involvement/enthusiasm for the party acceptable.) What exactly did von Bolschwing contribute to America after happily joining the SS in 1933 to make ignoring his crimes worthwhile? What's the purpose of this kind of grim revelation? There are several.

One, they diminish the moral high ground about the Second World War that the US clings to desperately to this day. Yes, everyone who isn't literally Adolph Hitler gets to feel pretty good about themselves, so anyone not allied with Hitler must be doing the right thing. Yet, helping to plan the Final Solution is forgivable if the CIA really wants you around. Another more contemporary reason to be horrified by this revelation is that it is just one outrage of many. Sharing the CIA's dark corner is most of the other big-name, secretive agencies. For the past 18 months, the National Security Agency's (NSA) massive campaign of spying has been big news. Less prominent were stories that suggest the Federal Bureau of Investigation (FBI) and Drug Enforcement Administration (DEA) are also playing the part of secretive, unaccountable rulers."

Welcome to the Reich, American Style

William Binney, former NSA employee and whistleblower, stated that the NSA had gone "totalitarian". In an interview with DW he likened the NSA and the US government to the Third Reich.

Binney: *"Sure, they haven't gone that far yet [as the Nazis and East German Stassi], but they tried to shut down newspaper reporters like Jim Risen...Look at the NDAA Section 1021, that gave President Obama the ability to define someone as a terrorist threat and have the military incarcerate them*

11

indefinitely without due process. That's the same as the special order 48 issued in 1933 by the Nazis, [the so-called Reichstag Fire Decree]. Read that – it says exactly the same thing. These were totalitarian processes that were instituted...Totalitarianism comes in the form first of knowledge of people and what they're doing, and then it starts to transition into using that power against people. That's what's happening – in terms of newspaper reporters, in terms of crimes. That is a direct violation of our constitution.

DW: But surely the difference is that there was an ideological regime behind the Stasi and the Nazis.

Binney: *You mean like putting people like John Kiriakou in prison for exposing torture and giving the torturers immunity? That's what our country is coming to. That's what we did. That is disgraceful. The motives of totalitarian states are not exactly the same every time, but they're very similar: power, control and money...We're focusing now on everyone on the planet – that's a change from focusing on organizations that were attempting to do nasty things. When you focus on everybody, you're moving down that path towards population control. "*

Ingeniously Produced from Concentration Camps: Data "Comes to Light"

Many advances in warfare can be traced to Nazi innovations built on the backs of tortured souls. For example, air and ship crew survivability in frigid seas is just one of them: *"...the Germans noted the terrible loss of critical personnel in sudden cold water immersion accidents. The sinking of the Bismarck and loss of airmen who bailed out alive and well into the cold North Sea during the Battle of Britain caused their physiologists and aviation medicine physicians to examine the problem. They commenced a large Research and Development program, which in part was the cause for the infamous Dachau experiments. They were the first to observe the "after drop" or continuation in reduction of body core temperature after being withdrawn from the cold water. They also experimented with survival suits and the Deutsches Textilforschunginstitut in München-Gladbach, ingeniously produced one that provided the insulation using soap bubbles which appears to have gone into limited service."*

Another example is the development of the military aircraft "ejection seat". In Achtung! Schleuder-Sitzaparat by Chris Carry, German engineering was far afield of American efforts in pilot safety. *"With the acquisition by the US of both German databases in egress research and actual examples of the German Heinkel explosive cartridge ejection seat immediately after the war had ended, the US began to vigorously attempt to gain greater knowledge in this overlooked area of aviation technology. The new American developmental research spurred on by acquisition of German wartime data branched off into two distinctly different approaches towards the same end, one taken by the US Air Force and one by the US Navy."*

Exceptionalism and Innovative Torture Techniques Led to Technological Advances

How could human beings engage in such hideous experiments on other human beings? Well, that is a time tested formula: Indoctrinate the masses into thinking that all others besides, say, Americans, are inferior, unexceptional, demons and insects. The world is witnessing just that as the US government, its allies and its media and academic proxies seek to reduce the Russians, Arabs, Chinese, Iranians, and the immigrants, unemployed and impoverished in the United States down to the level of parasitic microbes.

Just how does that mentality work?

For that answer we turn to the UK's Telegraph for an article written in 2008 by Richard Evans.

"The answer springs from the fact that medicine was both dominant in the world of science under the Third Reich, and closely allied to the Nazi project... After all, German medical science had uncovered the causes of several major diseases and contributed massively to improving the health of the population over the previous decades. Surely, therefore, it was justified in eliminating negative influences as well? What underpinned this behavior was a widespread belief that some people were less than human, relegated to a lower plane of existence by their inherited degeneracy – or their race. For German doctors, a camp inmate was either a racially inferior subhuman, a vicious criminal, a traitor to the German cause, or more than one of the above. Such beings had no right to life or wellbeing – indeed, it was logical that they should be sacrificed in the interests of the survival and triumph of the German race, just as that race had to be strengthened by the elimination of the inferior, degenerate elements within it."

Evans continues on describing the torture.

"SS doctors used inmates to test treatments for injuries sustained in battle, cutting open their calves and sewing bits of glass or wood or gauze impregnated with bacteria into the wounds, sometimes even smashing the prisoners' bones with hammers to create a more realistic effect; again, the results were presented to scientific conferences without anyone offering any criticism of the methods employed. Perhaps the

most enthusiastic user of human guinea pigs was the ambitious young SS doctor Sigmund Rascher, who employed camp inmates at Dachau to test the human body's reactions to rapid decompression and lack of oxygen, in an attempt to help pilots forced to parachute out of their planes at high altitudes. He called some of his research sessions "terminal experiments". He measured the time it took his subjects to die as their air supply was gradually thinned out. He showed his work, which led to the deaths of between 70 and 80 prisoners, to a conference of Luftwaffe medical experts in September 1942. The following month, Rascher presented the results of another experiment to a conference of 95 medical scientists in Nuremberg. This time, he showed how long inmates dressed in Luftwaffe uniforms and life jackets could survive in cold water, simulating conditions in the North Sea. The average time that elapsed before death, he reported, was 70 minutes. None of those listening to him raised any ethical objections."

Albert Camus offers a sort of prayer for these dark times.

"All I ask is that, in the midst of a murderous world, we agree to reflect on murder and to make a choice. After that, we can distinguish those who accept the consequences of being murderers themselves or the accomplices of murderers, and those who refuse to do so with all their force and being. Since this terrible dividing line does actually exist, it will be a gain if it be clearly marked. Over the expanse of five continents throughout the coming years an endless struggle is going to be pursued between violence and friendly persuasion, a struggle in which, granted, the former has a thousand times the chances of success than that of the latter.

US MILITARY'S PROGRESSIVENESS

But I have always held that, if he who bases his hopes on human nature is a fool, he who gives up in the face of circumstances is a coward. And henceforth, the only honorable course will be to stake everything on a formidable gamble--that words are more powerful than munitions."

US MILITARY'S PROGRESSIVENESS
American War Machine Ramping Up for Revenge: U.S.
Media Role is to Pacify the Nation

December 4, 2014: *"The most effectual engines for pacifying a nation are the public papers... A despotic government always keeps a kind of standing army of news-writers who, without any regard to truth or to what should be like truth, invent and put into the papers whatever might serve the ministers. This suffices with the mass of the people who have no means of distinguishing the false from the true paragraphs of a newspaper."* **Thomas Jefferson**

"Freedom of the press is another of the principal slogans of pure democracy...The capitalists have always use the term freedom to mean freedom for the rich to get richer and for the workers to starve to death. In capitalist usage freedom of the press means freedom of the rich to bribe the press and freedom to use their wealth to shape and fabricate so-called public opinion. In this respect, too, the defenders of pure democracy prove to be defenders of an utterly foul and venal system that gives the rich control over the mass media. They prove to be deceivers of the people, who, with the aid of plausible, fine-sounding, but thoroughly false phrases, divert them from the concrete historical task of liberating the press from capitalist enslavement..." **V.I. Lenin**

According to Stars & Stripes, United States Air Force Captain William Dubois—30 years old–was killed when the F-16 he was piloting on a mission against the Islamic State crashed. Marine Lance Cpl. Sean Neal, 19, of Riverside, California died in Iraq from a noncombat related injury. Marine Cpl. Jordan Spears, 21, of Memphis, Ind., was lost at sea while conducting flight operations in the North Arabian Gulf.

US MILITARY'S PROGRESSIVENESS
Does anyone care or even notice?

These deaths were part of Operation Inherent Resolve, the American military operation designed to eliminate the Islamic Caliphate and the Syrian government run by Bashar Assad. Operation Inherent Resolve is a minor sub-plot in the grand opera/geo-strategy of the United States of America. The final act of the geopolitical opera envisioned by the grand brains of the United States is to either contain or destabilize Russia and China, and corral the lesser BRICS (Brazil, India, and South Africa).

Over the past two decades the United States and Western Europe have been burned badly by the shoddy thinking of its strategists, economists, financiers, policy makers, politicians, academicians and military leaders.

They chose to sacrifice trillions of dollars (US) in treasure and millions of lives (soldiers, civilians killed, wounded, displaced) only to lose the wars in Iraq, Afghanistan, Syria, and Libya. They have created chaos in the Middle East/Persian Gulf apparently by design.

They stood idly by while Palestinian children were slaughtered by Israel. They clapped quietly as a military coup was undertaken in Egypt that restored the dictatorial status quo there meaning arms transfers and military cooperation could return to normal.

The Americans and West Europeans incited revolution in Ukraine and looked the other way as Nazi's brazenly assisted in the overthrow of a democratically elected government there. When Russia balked and seized Crimea the Americans and Europeans were embarrassingly out maneuvered. When China allowed Edward Snowden (NSA whistleblower) to leave Hong

Kong and Russia decided to allow him to stay in Russia, the Americans and Europeans were aghast at knowing they were, once again outmatched.

Further, the dunderheads in America and Western Europe finally succeeded in bringing an old Cold War nightmare to reality: their self-aggrandizing actions caused Russia and China to embrace in the form of economic and military trade deals that cut out the United States and Europe. Once again Russia has bested the Americans and Western Europeans by ditching the South Stream pipeline in favor of a pipeline to Turkey leaving Southern Europe in energy jeopardy.

Revenge!

In the cities and towns of the United States and Western Europe citizens are on edge about matters of life-security: employment, food, shelter, clothing, health insurance, education. Millions are unemployed or just culled from the statistical tables, forgotten. Children are going hungry. Immigrants are feeling the brunt of national anxiety/jingoism as they always do before street violence and war take place.

Class warfare is visible from the streets of Ferguson, Missouri to Detroit, Michigan. The classic hit song "Monster" by Steppenwolf sums it up: *"The cities have turned into jungles and corruption is strangling' the land. The police force is watching the people and the people just can't understand. We don't know how to mind our own business 'cause the whole world's got to be just like us. Now we are fighting a war over there, no matter who's the winner we can't pay the cost."* The United States of America can't even field a high speed bullet train.

Only a global economic and kinetic war is going to satiate the hunger for revenge that the top echelons of American and Western European leadership currently display.

American President Obama will initiate the big war and President Hillary Clinton will accelerate it. During the American presidential election all citizens will agree that the big war for American dominance is a given and not up for debate. The flood gates of cash will be opened by the US Congress even as social security and safety net benefits are slashed. It has all been decided in advance.

And now's the time for war! Who is going to cover the war for the masses? How will anyone really know what's going on?

Is it not genius that the media that would have provided the public with war news has been crippled through the prosecution and intimidation of journalists like James Risen, or of whistleblowers like John Kiriakou languishing in a federal prison? Then there is the collusion between the American government and media concerns like the New York Times which makes determining what is propaganda and actionable news difficult. The world knows that the US government, through the National Security Agency, is listening in: Those who might lead antiwar rebellions, or write contrarian reports, can be tracked and eliminated.

According to the Pew Research Journalism Project 25 percent of the 952 local television stations in the United States do not produce their own news products relying instead on contractors or sharing arrangements with third parties. Newsroom reductions in force continue across most mainstream media brands which–in spite of the hype over niche news outlets like Buzzfeed, Mashable, Politico, Vice News and Vox–still produce the bulk of the news products that Americans feed off of. And mainstream media continues to cut its news sectors. According to the Pew Research Journalism Project, "Full-time professional newsroom employment declined another 6.4% in 2012 with more losses expected for 2013. Gannett alone is estimated to have cut 400 newspaper jobs while the Tribune Co. announced 700 (not all of them in the newsroom)."

A clear and present danger to the reading, listening, feeling and seeing public is the growth of sponsored/biased journalism masking as news. Native advertising is a multibillion dollar industry and growing. Nearly every news organization in the United States is in on the game in which requiring journalists/reporters write with the sponsor/advertiser in mind, not the public and national interest.

Custom Propaganda

According to the Pew Research Journalism Project: "*The overlap between public relations and news noted in last year's State of the News Media report became even more pronounced. One of the greatest areas of revenue experimentation now involves website content that is paid for by commercial advertisers – but often written by journalists on staff – and placed on a news publishers' page in a way that sometimes makes it indistinguishable from a news story. Following the lead of early adapters like The Atlantic and Mashable, native advertising, as it is called by the industry, caught on rapidly in 2013. The New York Times, The Washington Post and most recently The Wall Street Journal have now begun or announced plans to begin devoting staff to this kind of advertising, often as a part of a new* "custom content division." eMarketer predicts that native ads spending will reach $2.85 billion by 2014. Many of these publishers initially expressed caution over such ads, with Wall Street Journal editor-in-chief Gerard Baker even describing it as a "Faustian pact." In the end, though, many publishers eventually came down with a conclusion similar to Baker's, who said that he was *"confident that our readers will appreciate what is sponsor-generated content and what is content from our global staff,"* according to a statement released by The Journal. *"That may be the case, and it could also be the case that stories created for and paid for by advertisers do not bother consumers as long as they are a good read. At this point, though, there is little if any public data that speak to consumer response one way or the other."*

A similar model has long been in operation with heavyweight think tanks like the Brookings Institution who receive funding from foreign sources/sponsors to, ultimately, influence policy makers in Washington, DC. Once again the notorious non-profit NGO's reveal their true colors: "Show us the money and we'll justify anything!

Perhaps the day will come when the pundits, journalists, think tank mavens, and retired war machine veterans will be required to dress like NASCAR or Formula One race car drivers whose clothing is littered with patches advertising this and that corporation/sponsor.

Mind, Soul and Dreams Owned by Disney, Comcast, Fox, CBS, Pearson

Do you spends hours watching television until you drift into sleep? Do you read a newspaper or magazine during breakfast or lunch? Do you frequent websites that only cater to your ideology? What feeds your mind and creates your identity?

Who, really, are you? It's an important question to ask yourself.

US MILITARY'S PROGRESSIVENESS

In the original Total Recall Arnold Schwarzenegger plays a character named Quaid. He thinks that he really is Quaid, a construction worker married to a beautiful wife played by the Sharon Stone. Events transpire that reveal Quaid is really Hauser, a sinister government agent (also played by Schwarzenegger) in collusion with the oppressive Governor Cohaagen of a Mars mining colony. After a violent encounter with Cohaagen's henchmen, Quaid discovers he has killing skills he was unaware of. A rough and tumble scene with Stone follows and ends with Stone revealing to Quaid: *"Your whole life is just a dream...implanted by 'the agency.'"*

Later Quaid comes to find out that he really is Hauser. This revelation comes via Hauser speaking to Quaid from a prerecorded video displayed on a laptop television: *"Hauser: Howdy, stranger! This is Hauser. If things have gone wrong, I'm talking to myself and you don't have a wet towel around your head. Now, whatever your name is, get ready for the big surprise. You are not you, you're me."*

Here is a sampling of the vertically integrated companies that make you not you, but them: Disney owns ABC News, ESPN, Touchstone Pictures, Marvel Comics, Cruise Lines, Hyperion Books and Reedy Energy Services. Comcast owns NBC Universal, the Philadelphia Flyers, and is attempting to acquire Time Warner Cable. Fox News Corporation owns the Dow Jones & Company (Wall Street Journal, Barron's, DJX, etc.), Harper Collins Publishers, Move, Inc. (real estate news), 20th Century Fox, Fox News Channel, and Amplify (educational products for K-12). CBS owns Simon & Schuster, CNET, the Smithsonian Network, and 130 radio stations. Time Warner owns CNN, Time magazine, HBO, MAX, Sports Illustrated Kids, and People Magazine. Pearson influences the course of American education through its publishing houses, digital learning platforms, and a 50 percent interest in the Economist Magazine, Penguin Random House and the Financial Times.

Millions of 19, 21 and 30 year olds—civilians and not–are going to going to be killed, maimed, wounded and displaced in the coming years. Try to find out why.

America's Sorrowful World: Dumb at Home and Dumber Abroad

April 21, 2015: *"I should tell you that homosexuality in our country has been overcome once and for all but not entirely. Or entirely but not completely. Or else entirely and completely but not once and for all. What do people think about now? Nothing but homosexuality. That and the Middle East, Israel, the Golan Heights. Moshe Dayan. So, if they chase Moshe Dayan off the Golan Heights and the Arabs make peace with the Jews? Nothing but homosexuality pure and simple."*
(Moscow to the End of the Line, Venedikt Erofeev, 1969)

"And freedom thus remains a phantom on that continent of sorrow [the United States of America] and the people, thus, have become so used to it that they almost don't notice...On every rotten face there is as much dignity expressed in a minute as would last us for our whole great Seven Year Plan. How come? I thought, and turned off Manhattan onto Fifth Avenue and answered my own question. Because of their vile self-satisfaction—nothing else. But where do they get their self-satisfaction? I froze in the middle of the Avenue in order to resolve the thought: In the world of propagandistic fictions and advertising vagaries, where do they get their self-satisfaction? I was heading into Harlem and shrugged my shoulders. Where? The playthings of monopoly's ideologues, the marionettes of the arms kings, where do they get such appetite? They gorge five times a day and always with the same endless dignity—but can a man have a real appetite in the States?"
(Moscow to the End of the Line, Venedikt Erofeev, 1969)

US MILITARY'S PROGRESSIVENESS
Media Stooges Analyze Three Stooges Methodology

The ghastly spectacle of presidential debates on issues overly cooked in the media for decades (Israel and sexual preference, for example) will befall Americans within the blink of an eye. Of course they are not debates but well-rehearsed professional theater with the candidates, media questioners and audiences all acting out their assigned roles, on queue. Who has the appetite for it all? It is a hollow, unreal process and a rather sickening charade unless one is on some measure of hallucinogenic drug or drunk. At the proper stage of hallucination or inebriation the show turns into a sort of Looney Tunes cartoon making the time spent on the theater that is the American presidential election process somewhat tolerable.

A few more hits or swigs are necessary to endure the post-debate commentary on Fox, CNN, CBS, PBS or ABC. Depending on the mind altering substance used, the airhead punditry takes on the persona of the Three Stooges/Tractor Pull announcers. Caked in makeup and attached by wireless earphone to assistants who tell them what to say—the talking heads try to convince the audience that what they saw/heard was not what they saw/heard: In short, they try to spin sense on the nonsense uttered by this and that candidate. The media stooges extol the glorious exceptionalism of democratic style and process of the American presidential election process-and US elections in general—as though no other nation on earth actually holds elections.

US MILITARY'S PROGRESSIVENESS
Scary Monster

Americans know (or should know) that the presidential candidates–like all US politicians—have brains made of Silly Putty. They are bent and molded by the interests that fund them and, of course, tell them how to think/vote. Yet the American voting public typically runs a fool's errand every four years with the false notion that "voting matters". Voters proudly place stickers on ties and lapels stating an in-your-face "I Voted!" as if that is some sort of intellectual badge of courage that matters. But it doesn't when the Democrats and Republicans are a sort of two-headed Grendel hungry for money and power.

It's a well fed monster that works on behalf of those political and military leaders who designed the carnage underway in Iraq, Syria, Yemen, Libya and Afghanistan and seek more. Displaced human beings in those countries seeking a non-violent life and some measure of security to practice their faith (Christian, Sunni, and Shia) have been forced to flee their long-time homes due to war and the reprisals it brings. There are millions of displaced now. They drown at sea, are slaughtered by splinter groups like ISIS and Al Qaeda or by errant air strikes courtesy of US targeting intelligence or US military hardware sold to the likes of Saudi Arabia.

The story in the USA is dismal in its own way: Austerity, local law enforcement gunning down unarmed suspects; the Supreme Court through Citizens United opening the floodgates for corporate cash donations to political candidates; a bankruptcy judge in Detroit, Michigan claiming that clean water is not a "right"; drought in the state of California; one in three US children living in poverty; and the slashing of funding for Social Security and Medicare. These woes do not include the unemployed culled from government statistics, homelessness, or the care and cost of taking care of Americans returning from battlefields the world over. And yet some lunatics in the USA still want to go to war with Iran, Russia and China.

And go figure! The USA is a country with 243 million adults 18 and over, and is indoctrinated from an early age by its educational system to believe, nearly religiously, in an open competitive market, based on an equally competitive democratic/economic system of government. Yet in the current presidential cycle the USA can only produce two viable presidential candidates who just so happen to represent America's wealthiest and political powerful families: Hillary Clinton (Democrat) and Jeb Bush (Republican). The two families are so close that George W. Bush called Bill Clinton "the brother from another mother." Both campaigns combined will likely spend $5 billion dollars on a science fiction movie titled The 2016 Presidential Swindle.

Dumb it down for the People

So how do the policy makers, military leaders, corporate heads, pollsters, pundits and campaign managers see the American public?

Consider Michael Glennon, Tufts University Fletcher School, and author of Double Government, on the intellectual ability of the American public. Turns out the American public mind is one giant mass of Silly Putty! "...*the economic and educational realities remain stark [in the USA]. Nearly 50 million Americans—more than 16% of the population and almost 20% of American children—live in poverty. A 2009 federal study estimated that thirty-two million American adults,*

28

about one in seven, are unable to read anything more challenging than a children's picture book and are unable to understand the side effects of medication listed on a pill bottle. The Council on Foreign Relations reported that the United States has 'slipped ten spots in both high school and college graduation rates over the past three decades.' One poll found that nearly 25% of Americans do not know that the United States declared its independence from Great Britain. A 2011 Newsweek survey disclosed that 80% did not know who was president during World War I; 40% did not know who the United States fought in World War II; 29% could not identify the current Vice President of the United States; 70% did not know that the Constitution is the supreme law of the land; 65% did not know what happened at the constitutional convention; 88% could not identify any of the writers of the Federalist Papers; 27% did not know that the President is in charge of the Executive Branch; 61% did not know the length of a Senate term; 81% could not name one power conferred on the federal government by the Constitution; 59% could not name the Speaker of the House; and 63% did not know how many justices are on the Supreme Court.

Far more Americans can name the Three Stooges than any member of the Supreme Court. Other polls have found that 71% of Americans believe that Iran already has nuclear weapons and that 33% believed in 2007 that Saddam Hussein was personally involved in the 9/11 attacks. In 2006, at the height of U.S. military involvement in the region, 88% of American 18- to 24- year-olds could not find Afghanistan on a map of Asia, and 63% could not find Iraq or Saudi Arabia on a *map of the Middle East. Three quarters could not find Iran or Israel, and 70% could not find North Korea. The 'over-vote' ballots of several thousand voters—greater in number than the margin of difference between George W. Bush and Al Gore—were rejected in Florida in the 2000 presidential election because voters did not understand that they could vote for only one candidate. There is, accordingly, little need for purposeful deception to induce generalized deference…in contemporary America…President Harry Truman's Secretary of State Dean Acheson, not renowned for bluntness, let slip his own similar assessment of America's electorate. 'If you truly had a democracy and did what the people wanted,' he said, 'you'd go wrong every time.' Acheson's views were shared by other influential foreign policy experts, as well as government officials; thus emerged America's 'efficient' national security institution."*

Who cares? That's the way it is. It is what it is. It has always been this way. Nothing you can do about it.

"People don't see clearly unless they want to. Nowadays everyone quietly accepts the inevitable. Newspapers are no help, they censored themselves little by little until they perfected the art of saying absolutely nothing. Television is monitored by official censors. Even if it weren't monitored there is nothing on of interest. The news bulletins are completely innocuous…How can anyone believe a word these officials say?" **(And Still the Earth, Ignacio De Loyola Brandao, 1985)**

The United States is surely becoming a continent of sorrow.

US MILITARY'S PROGRESSIVENESS
The American Dream: Designed by War Planners

May 10, 2015: *"It is wrong to believe that postwar American suburbanization prevailed because the public chose it...Suburbanization prevailed because of the decisions of large operators and powerful economic institutions supported by federal government programmes...ordinary consumers had little real choice in the basic pattern that resulted...Essentially city planners saw the atomic threat as a means to accelerate the trend of suburbanization. Plans to circle American cities with open spaces, highways and circumferential life belts was long overdue...The federal government played a more effective role in reducing urban vulnerability [to atomic attack] in future residential development by working through the Federal Housing Administration [FHA], The Housing and Home Finance Agency and the Federal National Mortgage Association [FNMA]. As the FHA and the FNMA annually guaranteed federal liability for hundreds of thousands of dwelling units, the federal government could mandate that in the future they all be subject to urban defense standards."* **The Reduction of Urban Vulnerability: Revisiting 1950s American Suburbanization as Civil Defence, Kathleen A. Tobin**

Turns out the "American Dream" of owning a couple of automobiles and a home with cable television in the greener pastures of the suburbs was/is, in good measure, a national security matter. The homes beyond the city center that Americans live in and the highways they cruise are all the result, directly or indirectly, of a national defense program that planers hoped would ensure the existential survivability of America.

US MILITARY'S PROGRESSIVENESS

Making it tougher for the "Reds", or these days' terrorists, to figure out how to vaporize the critical functional elements of America's national power by dispersing centralized populations/industries to the suburbs was deemed critical to US Cold-War federal, state and local planners, and their counterparts in industry.

The United States government actively promoted the long term urban dispersal of its populations and industries because of the threat of nuclear annihilation by the, then, USSR. Immediately following World War II and throughout the 1950's, publications like the Bulletin of Atomic Scientists carried the views of prominent officials/academicians who vigorously argued for the dispersal of populations and industries located in major cities throughout the United States. The idea was not to eliminate the urban center but to expand and stretch its radius to such an extent that it would make it more difficult for the "Godless Commies" to pick and choose targets that mattered. In short, city limits would become meaningless.

As a result of the largely successful national defense efforts at urban dispersal in the 1950's, today's opponents (Russia, China, terrorists) planning a nuclear attack on, say, the Pentagon in Arlington County, Virginia—and defense industrial base office sites that surround it—know that it would be merely a symbolic act as US military command and control functions, and defense manufacturing sites, are not centralized but scattered all over the Washington—Baltimore Metropolis.

(Deborah Natsios' National Security SPRAWL: Washington, DC provides one of the premier studies of the after-effect of urban dispersal/suburbanization planning based on national defense requirements. Find it at the Cryptome website.

US MILITARY'S PROGRESSIVENESS

The threat of nuclear war and the argument for urban dispersal/suburbanization of the American populace had other positive aspects accruing to the US homeland. According to Tobin's work, "Indirectly the atomic bomb offered a rare opportunity for greatly improving the living conditions of millions of our citizens. Our large cities have been growing larger, resulting in more crowded streets and tenement homes…If [dispersal] is done properly, we will at the same time greatly increase our urban attractiveness."

Who knew that urban renewal and building codes were based, in part, on the need for defense against nuclear weapons?

Dream On: No Free Will, No Free Market

There is a lot of bluster about the free and open market that is supposed to exist in the Western World, in particular in the United States. Senior officials revolving in and out of the federal government and the commercial sector are very fond of promoting the benefits of privatization, deregulation and the invisible hand of the free market which, allegedly, magically sets prices, encourages or discourages competition, and provides consumers free choice in the selection of hard and soft goods.

That is a really big lie.

It is the US federal government, and its national defense dollars, that has stimulated the development of nearly every single technological innovation during and since World War II. It was federal tax breaks/subsidies, federal low interest or secured loans, and federal funding for research and development that prompted an otherwise risk averse, stodgy US private sector to commercialize and produce the products that American war-makers, warfighters and consumers now take for granted.

The lives–individually and collectively–that Americans lead have, in many ways, been planned and designed for them by the realities of war and the necessity to prepare for it. That life has been sold to them through slick advertising/marketing campaigns equating freedom with consumption and production. Such are the foundations of American capitalist democracy along with the necessity to pry open—and exploit–new global markets with a military can opener. These harsh realities must be buried in distracting consumption of things that distract citizens from recognizing reality.

According to American Capitalism and its Effects, *"People in consumerist societies live by the influence of advertisements, and often methodically buy things they do not need, and in most cases, cannot afford. This, in turn, leads to greater economic disparity, and despite having the most or latest products, consumerists have a feeling of unfulfillment due to spending a lot of money, yet having nothing of personal importance."*

It is a tough thought for any American to bear in mind. At least it should be. Less than six degrees of separation removes an American from some product or service that originated from the national defense imperative.

Unmanned Aerial Vehicles/Drones, The Internet, the World Wide Web, Radar and Laser technology, Synthetic Rubber/Oil/Nylon, Digital Computers, Nuclear Power, Cell Phones, Jet Engines, Rocket/Launch technology and dozens of other innovations were born thanks to the US federal government. In War Play by Corey Mead (an essential read!),

US MILITARY'S PROGRESSIVENESS

we learn that video games and distance learning were also born of national defense needs, not some geek or guru tinkering in a garage in America's hinterlands. Mead's work also shows how much America's elite universities depend on US federal/military funds: Harvard, MIT and Johns Hopkins among them.

No wonder the US national security community, most recognizably the uniformed military services, are increasingly deified by the American public and viewed with the awe reserved for the Gods. As organized religion has faded in America, the new religion of militarism has ascended.

It makes perfect sense as it was programmed by national defense planners long ago into the sequence that is the American Dream.

The Masses as Goats and Dogs: Townsend and Sade's Doctrines Rule the World

June 19, 2015: *"The citizens whose lives are split between business and private life, their private life between ostentation and intimacy, their intimacy between the sullen community of marriage and the bitter solace of being entirely alone, at odds with themselves and with everyone, are virtually already Nazis who are at once enthusiastic and fed up or the city dwellers of today who can imagine friendship only as a social contract between the inwardly connected."* **The Dialectic of Enlightenment, Max Horkheimer and Theodor Adorno (1944).**

"The religious chimeras must be replaced by the utmost terrors. The people must be freed from the fear of a future Hell. Once that is destroyed they will abandon themselves to anything. But the chimerical law must be replaced by penal laws of enormous severity which apply of course only to the people since they alone cause unrest in the state.... What do the rich care for the idea of a leash they will never feel themselves if this empty semblance gives them the right to grind down those living under its yoke?" **Horkheimer and Adorno quoting from Juliette by the Marquis de Sade (1797).**

The founders and practitioners of free-market ideology have finally succeeded in turning the individual intellect, and the collective that is Western civilization, into little more than value-objects. Now, all are witness to the reality that everything, everyone, every emotion and even every movement has a price and a cost. Western society and individual thought has, at long last, become totally materialistic; which is to say, completely economic according to practices decidedly informed by 18th, 19th Century philosophy (often misinformed).

All manner of life from the quanta of action to the intimacy of lovers is irretrievably locked into economic value functions. This has led to the ice cold calculus, and equally brutal callousness, now present in the minds of the rulers, and the ruled, which sees transgender and transracial issues; Greek financial woes; job liquidation and unemployment; private and public pension pillaging; cuts in social safety nets (austerity); head transplants; and; for example, US preparations for open war in/or with Syria, Iraq, Russia and China as natural and as expected as the sun's presence during the day. No emotion of care or concern arises that would see even a finger lifted to change the system as it is as such.

What's the Point?

The efforts of journalists and academics are nearly intellectually bankrupt save for the "effort" of trying to report on the world not as it appears, but as it is as designed and managed by a willful economic totalitarianism that provides for a "free" life in terms demanded by economic doctrine, even as it tortures that life daily, providing no escape from the daily routine. Even dreams are polluted.

The intellectual limits of the unenhanced human mind have now been reached. Is it any wonder that technological, bioengineering and chemical enhancements are rapidly being called for by all?

This is not a beyond-Capitalism, Marxist play in operation. It is, rather, the emergence and acceptance of economic, social and cultural Sadism that has now been blessed, purchased and brought into the service of the market economy. The most puzzling forms of human behavior, and their most horrifying, are no longer repulsive or indignant, or hampered in their development, production and marketing. They are valuable in the sense that they are held by society to have monetary value either in the form of debt or credit. Such is the replacement for the concepts of right and wrong, moral and immoral. Boundaries and limits have been eliminated in every sphere of life.

In the era of transgender and transracial one can only expect that trans-life will be next.

Religion and family offer no refuge now having been shocked and awed into defeat by the necessities of the free-market imperative, and the practices and myths they offered which have decisively been ridiculed and defeated by the new religion of the free-market. Christ's sacrifice no longer matters. Now the view is that Christ was a fool and the Father a nut to sacrifice his only Son. Besides, Paternalism, like all "Western Whiteness", is not part of humanity's historical process, but resident evil on Earth. Even here the industries of Diversity have been compromised by the sacraments of "buy and sell" as even they must earn their daily bread.

There is nothing current in 21st Century academia or journalism that addresses the Sadistic now which has become a perpetual moment-in-motion in which history is despised for its reality and the future lies someplace in the fantasy notions of a pre-history. Perhaps humanity's fate is a pre-history.

Robert Townsend's Animal Kingdom

Who knew that goats and dogs were so important to the development of today's economic practice?

"...Malthus and Darwin owed their inspiration to this source [Townsend's goats/dogs, see below]. Malthus learned of it from Condorcet, Darwin from Malthus. Yet neither Darwin's theory of natural selection nor Malthus' population laws might have exerted any appreciable influence on modern society but for the maxims which Townsend deduced from his goats and dogs and wished to have applied to the reform of the poor law...Here was a new starting point for political science. By approaching human community from the animal side, Townsend bypassed the supposedly unavoidable question as to the foundation of government and in so doing introduced a new concept of law into human affairs–that of the laws of nature."
The Great Transformation, Karl Polanyi (1944).

In this excerpt from A Dissertation on the Poor Laws, by Robert Townsend (1786), the masses get vilified by a well-to-do Englishman. When reading Townsend it is important to note, as Polanyi points out, that in the United Kingdom at the time, poor meant anyone who did not have the wealth to be leisurely 24/7. Just 15 percent of those in the United Kingdom were allowed to vote at the time.

"The poor know little of the motives which stimulate the higher ranks to action-pride, honor, and ambition. In general it is only hunger which can spur and goad them on to labor...Who is *most worthy to suffer cold and hunger, the prodigal or the provident, the slothful or the diligent, the virtuous or the vicious? In the South Seas there is an island, which from the first discoverer is called Juan Fernandez. In this sequestered spot, John Fernando placed a colony of goats, consisting of one male, attended by his female. This happy couple finding pasture in abundance, could readily obey the first commandment, to increase and multiply, till in process of time they had replenished their little island. In advancing to this period they were strangers to misery and want, and seemed to glory in their numbers: but from this unhappy moment they began to suffer hunger; yet continuing for a time to increase their numbers, had they been endued with reason, they must have apprehended the extremity of famine. In this situation the weakest first gave way, and plenty was again restored...partial evil was universal good.*

When the Spaniards found that the English privateers resorted to this island for provisions, they resolved on the total extirpation of the goats, and for this purpose they put on shore a greyhound dog and bitch. These in their turn increased and multiplied, in proportion to the quantity of food they met with; but in consequence, as the Spaniards had foreseen, the breed of goats diminished. Had they been totally destroyed, the dogs likewise must have perished. But as many of the goats retired to the craggy rocks, where the dogs could never follow them, descending only for short intervals to feed with fear and circumspection in the rallies, few of these, besides the careless and the rash, became a prey; and none but the most watchful, strong, and active of the dogs could get a sufficiency of food. Thus a new kind of balance was established. The weakest of both species were among the first to pay the debt of nature; the most active and vigorous preserved their lives. It is the quantity of food which regulates the numbers of the human species..."

The Genius of the Marquis

"Individuals in having to fend for themselves develop the ego as the agency of reflective foresight and overview; over successive generations it expands and contracts with the individuals prospects of economic autonomy and productive ownership. Finally it passes from the expropriated citizens to the totalitarian trust-masters whose science has become the

quintessence of the methods for the subjugation of the masses of society. Sade erected an early monument to their planning skills. The conspiracy of rulers against peoples implemented by relentless organization finds the enlightenment period no less compliant than the bourgeois republic. That spirt is hostile only to authority when authority lacks the strength to enforce obeisance and to violence only when violence is not an established fact. As long as one does not ask who is applying it, reason has no greater affinity with violence or mediation...it presents as peace or war, tolerance or repression as the given state of affairs...Reason as a purely formal entity is in the service of every natural interest. Becoming simply an organ, thinking reverts to nature. For the rulers, however, human beings become mere material as the whole of nature has become material for society." **(Horkheimer & Adorno)**

American Defense Secretary Ashton Carter: Physicist for War and Profit

June 24, 2015: *"Most Americans apply a yardstick to America's actions which is very different from the yardstick they apply to Russia's actions. Whenever their bias in favor of their own nation gets into conflict with the truth, the odds are that the bias will prevail. As a result of this they are not capable of seeing current events in their historical perspective…In Washington, wisdom has no chance to prevail at this point…If we intend to drop bombs on Russia in case of war, and expect Russia to drop bombs on us…then our threat to drop bombs on Russia is tantamount to murder and suicide."*
Leo Szilard: Are We On The Road To War? (1961)

The US defense secretary, Ashton Carter, is the face of much that is troublesome in Washington, DC. But he is "Mr. Right" for the varied capital interests and ideologies he represents: the fusion of neoliberalism and neo-conservatism; state sponsored corporate welfare; the revolving door; opportunism and greed; the "free market"; and a science and technology that is first and foremost in the service of weapons and war.

Carter has absolutely nothing in common with the rank and file of the military (those at the tip-of-the spear) who he ostensibly is supposed to represent.

"Ash" is a one percent guy, representing the one or so percent that moves and shakes the classes that make up society like the puppeteer does marionettes. Carter's primary interest is in further privatizing, and eliminating, the State's role in national security for the purpose of providing more profit opportunities for defense contractors and weapons research laboratories. Through his DIUx initiative that aims to leech off hi-tech commercial industry, he is pushing the tentacles of the Pentagon deeper into the private sector. Makes sense, one guesses, since the US is in a midst of a war that will never end, or will not be allowed to end.

The honorable US defense secretary studied physics, receiving his PhD from Oxford. His specialty was quantum chromodynamics, a field of study in which two of the giants of 20th Century physics, Nobel Laureates Richard Feynman and Murray Gell-Mann, set the pace. Carter opted to pursue the profitable path of science and technology in the service of weapons and war, and the individuals and organizations that design strategies and technologies that require that America remain in a perpetual state of war of some kind.

Carter, and like-minded technocrats seeking to cozy up to global capital and power, has achieved a measure of wealth and fame over the years parlaying his technical and interpersonal acumen (contacts) in halls of government and in board rooms to maximum advantage for himself and vested interests. The Project on Government Oversight's piece on Carter titled "Taking the Revolving Door to a Whole New Level" is illuminating in this regard. Carter is certainly no Leo Szilard (founder of the Council for a Livable World and heavyweight 20th Century physicist) being more in the mold of Edward Teller, a strident supporter of missile defense systems.

"...Carter's role, like that of many other members of Washington's defense policy establishment, went deeper. While working in the private sector, he has held plum positions on government advisory boards that called for reforms with potential ramifications for his defense industry clients and other companies that receive DoD dollars...Carter's investment colleagues at Global Technology Partners included

other former senior officials—such as former Secretary of Defense William Perry and former CIA Director John Deutch— who were serving simultaneously as advisers to DoD. Perry and Deutch also had close ties to giant defense contractors: Perry served on the boards of UTC and Boeing, while Deutch served on the board of Raytheon.

From 1997 to 2001, Carter also served as a member of the Defense Policy Board, another influential Pentagon committee that advises on 'issues central to strategic Department of Defense (DoD) planning,' according to its charter. Unlike the Defense Science Board, the Defense Policy Board "does not publish separate reports,' according to a database of federal advisory committees, and it's unclear what role Carter played in the panel's work. Nonetheless, Carter's industry clients stood to benefit from his role as a Pentagon advisor on both panels. (Another former member of the Defense Policy Board, Richard Perle, ended up resigning after a controversy erupted over his ties to companies that had business pending before the government.)"

At the time of Global Technology Partners (GTP) press release/announcement of the alliance with Rothschild, besides Perry and Deutch, GTP key staff included former Pentagon undersecretary of defense for technology John Kaminski and John White, former Pentagon deputy defense secretary.

Carter, according to the document on the GTP-Rothschild alliance, was listed as having this expertise: "…a Senior Partner of Global Technology Partners, LLC. From 1993 to 1996, Dr. Carter served as U.S. Assistant Secretary of Defense for International Security Policy, with responsibility for formulating U.S. policy towards Russia and other states of the former Soviet Union, proliferation of weapons of mass destruction worldwide, arms control negotiations, and oversight of the U.S. nuclear arsenal and missile defense programs. He is also the former Chairman of the NATO High Level Group."

Carter is well positioned, for the benefit of current and former clients—to include the next president of the United States (Republican or Democrat)–to lead the charge against Russia and China. As the Project for Government Oversight pointed out, Carter has been a champion of missile defense technology and deployment for decades. Let's turn, in contrast to Carter, to Murray Gell-Mann, a physicist who worked on anti-ballistic missile defense systems in the 1960s. He concluded that they would be destabilizing. "A*nd the conclusions were very negative, that is, that it [ABM] would drastically reduce our security, and that we would be much better off if both the United States and the Soviet Union refrained from deploying significant ABM systems...*" Fast forward to 2015 and the issues central to the deployment of ABM systems, or missile defense systems, remains largely unchanged: escalation to defeat the defensive system always ensues.

Gell-Mann, and Szilard, acutely recognized the fragility of the planet and the human race. They knew, having seen first-hand the destructive power at humanity's disposal, that shortsightedness and narrowly defined interests—unchecked– will kill or alter the species beyond recognition. "*...what* might, *what the human race might do to achieve greater sustainability in the course of the twenty-first century, which is when it really has to happen, because now is the time when we've reached the inflection point in total human population and the rate of increase is beginning to decrease. It's the time when we've reached the stage where human beings can make changes of order one in the whole globe, whether through unwise*

45

US MILITARY'S PROGRESSIVENESS

economic activity or through destructive war; and this is clearly the time when if a set of transitions to a more sustainable world is to occur, they must occur," said Gell-Mann.

US MILITARY'S PROGRESSIVENESS
Neoliberal American Capitalism Rocks On! But Does Anyone Hear Pope Francis?

July 22, 2015: Though not explicitly stated, America's most powerful instrument of national power is Capitalism. The pistons that power Neoliberal American Capitalism are: Diplomacy, Information, Military, Economic, Financial, Law Enforcement, Intelligence and Human Capital/People. The clearest exposition of the instruments of national power on record can be found in the US Army's 2008 Special Operations Forces Unconventional Warfare Manual.

No assessment of American political, economic, international, cultural or military strategy/action can be stamped "legitimate" without reference to and understanding of these Olympian tools of power that America's leaders have at their disposal. Combined they are the elements that form the spear and its tip that is Neoliberal American Capitalism.

Iran's recent agreement with the Capitalized world would not have been possible without US leadership: That unseen collective of America's elite (representing all the interests of the instruments of national power) that seems to have finally understood how to calibrate America's instruments of national power to secure the nation's own interests and not those of Saudi Arabia and Israel.

More importantly, the Iran and Cuba deals represent only a small chunk of viral code in the larger American software program that seeks to undermine Russia's regional power and China's global designs. Neoliberal American Capitalism's addiction for markets and profit, or simply the sport of destabilizing countries, needs a constant fix. Drama aside, the

BRICS, and their bank pose an economic and financial threat to American national power.

With Iran (and Cuba) now willingly, and with a sense of urgency, opening their economies and cultures to Neoliberal American Capitalism, President Obama has, at last, a worthy legacy which consigns two of the remnants of American Cold War Capitalism to the grave and alters the geopolitical landscape in America's favor.

How can one not applaud and give credit to Obama and his Secretary of State John Kerry?

And Obama has been gracious in his diplomatic victory. Russia's role in facilitating the successful Iran agreement was acknowledged as critical despite the Pentagon's saber rattling (score one for the civil in civil-military relations). According to NBC News, *"President Barack Obama telephoned Russian President Vladimir Putin ...to thank him for his part in the recent nuclear deal with Iran, the White House said. The President thanked President Putin for Russia's important role in achieving this milestone, the culmination of nearly 20 months of intense negotiations, the White House said in a statement. It added that Obama and Putin agreed to remain in close touch as the Iran deal is implemented and would work together to reduce tensions in the Middle East, particularly in Syria. Russia was one of the six major powers that negotiated the deal reached with Iran on Tuesday in Vienna. The others were the United States, Germany, the European Union, China, Britain and France."*

Powerful forces in the USA/Israel and Iran would have gleefully sent generations of American and Iranian youth to their deaths had President Obama not "gone to the hoop" for an Iran deal.

So now it is time for the knuckle-draggers in Iran, Israel and the USA to cause general nausea by appearing in print and electronic media drunk on the noxious brew that leads them to oppose Iran deal. They will be joined by conspiracy mongers at the ready to yell "False Flag Operation!" "The circus is in town folks! In this ring the presidential contenders. Over in that ring the knuckle-heads and the conspiracy loons." The mainstream media will keep the circus alive until having run out of angles, it is forced to read sentences backwards.

Guns and Roses

So it has come to pass that Capitalism—the freedom to buy and sell goods, services, souls and the environment—was essentially the foundation upon which was built entryways for Iran and Cuba to become full members of globalized, networked world created largely by the United States after World War II.

What further can be written by the world's social activists about the ruthlessness of the monster that is Capitalism? Certainly it must always be challenged and critiqued. Who doesn't dream of developing an alternative that provides real life-security for all? But the world has to wonder if the human species is capable of creating an economic doctrine, a mystical religion, a science, or a secular philosophy that is not based on Capitalist motives and practice? Is Capitalism—whether American, Chinese, Russian, Brazilian, Turkish, et al, the only viable template for human existence? This is not to praise or bury Capitalism, or proclaim any historical end, but to coldly recognize that at the moment human interests seem best and precariously served by the constant near disasters that Capitalism engenders. And the odd fact is this: No one located at the high, medium or low points of society really knows what's going on. The human species is a Doctor Jekyll and Mr. Hyde construct which appears to be why Capitalism seems the right fit for whatever personality is in charge.

Perhaps Capitalism is "all we've got." It seems to have not reached its zenith particularly with the USA firmly at the helm of the good ship Capital and regaining speed. And what American—even the most vociferous anti-Capitalist really wants to see her country's instruments of national power eroded? No American honestly seeks second place just as no Russian, Chinese or Vietnamese chooses, when cornered, to dismiss his own nation's national interests. Pride and Capitalism are borne of the same substance.

As the kick-ass rock group Guns and Roses once sang, "Where do we go now?

Scarface Returns to Cuba

The normalization of relations with Cuba was really a classic no-brainer. The US and Cuba have a long history. Thomas Jefferson, commenting in 1820, thought that the absorption of Cuba by the USA would be a "most interesting" addition.

Losing market share and political influence to the emergent BRICS is no laughing matter. With few markets left on the planet to target and exploit, every billion US dollar's count. So Cuba's lousy economic performance can be ignored, and is. According to Reuters, China and Cuba's trade accounted for $1.4 billion in 2014. Russia TV reports that Russia's Rosneft energy concern is working with a Cuban oil company to seek out what is believed to be 20 billion barrels of oil of Cuba's coast. In 2013 Brazil and Cuba's trade was estimated at $625 million and, more significantly, Brazil is funding and constructing a deep water port at Mariel, Cuba which will be the key port of import/export of goods—and tourists–from Capitalists the world over, according to the Los Angeles Times.

Established in 1994 the US-Cuba Trade and Economic Council described the Cuban market this way: "...*the Republic of Cuba, 93 miles south of the United States, a nation of 11 million consumers, which would rank it the 7th largest state if the country were a part of the United States...*" That's big money if one can get in on it quick.

Heed the Pope's Warning

Amidst the wonders and miracles of Neoliberal American Capitalism that proponents never tire of proclaiming, there is the disease of constant crisis that plagues the market. Capitalists, of course, know that people and the ecological system (the planet) are the source of this disease. The brightest Capitalist would sooner cull the population through war and austerity rather than plant capital back into enterprises that create life-security, particularly for the young of this world.

There is only one global leader on this planet who knows this reality and actually has the guts to say it out loud in speeches in front of vast crowds and in quieter places like the Vatican website.

That guy is Pope Francis, the famed Jesuit and former bouncer, who serves as the world's "warning label" for the dangerous medicine that is Capitalism. He is encouraging young people the world over to "change the system" not unlike Malcolm X did in a speech at the Oxford Union in 1964.

US MILITARY'S PROGRESSIVENESS

We ignore Pope Francis at our own peril. It is worth reading, again, some excerpts from the pontiff's concerns about the planet.

The Pope's thoughts match up nicely with those in the Pale Blue Dot by Carl Sagan (search Pale Blue Dot on the Web).

Pope Francis: *Nowadays, for example, we are conscious of the disproportionate and unruly growth of many cities, which have become unhealthy to live in, not only because of pollution caused by toxic emissions but also as a result of urban chaos, poor transportation, and visual pollution and noise. Many cities are huge, inefficient structures, excessively wasteful of energy and water. Neighborhoods, even those recently built, are congested, chaotic and lacking in sufficient green space. We were not meant to be inundated by cement, asphalt, glass and metal, and deprived of physical contact with nature. In some places, rural and urban alike, the privatization of certain spaces has restricted people's access to places of particular beauty. In others, ecological neighborhoods have been created which are closed to outsiders in order to ensure an artificial tranquility. Frequently, we find beautiful and carefully manicured green spaces in so-called "safer" areas of cities, but not in the more hidden areas where the disposable of society live.*

The social dimensions of global change include the effects of technological innovations on employment, social exclusion, an inequitable distribution and consumption of energy and other services, social breakdown, increased violence and a rise in new forms of social aggression, drug trafficking, growing drug use by young people, and the loss of identity. These are signs that the growth of the past two centuries has not always led to an integral development and an improvement in the quality of life. Some of these signs are also symptomatic of real social decline, the silent rupture of the bonds of integration and social cohesion. Furthermore, when media and the digital world become omnipresent, their influence can stop people from learning how to live wisely, to think deeply and to love generously.

In this context, the great sages of the past run the risk of going unheard amid the noise and distractions of an information overload. Efforts need to be made to help these media become sources of new cultural progress for humanity and not a threat to our deepest riches. True wisdom, as the fruit of self-examination, dialogue and generous encounter between persons, is not acquired by a mere accumulation of data which eventually leads to overload and confusion, a sort of mental pollution. Real relationships with others, with all the challenges they entail, now tend to be replaced by a type of internet communication which enables us to choose or eliminate relationships at whim, thus giving rise to a new type of contrived emotion which has more to do with devices and displays than with other people and with nature. Today's media do enable us to communicate and to share our knowledge and affections. Yet at times they also shield us from direct contact with the pain, the fears and the joys of others and the complexity of their personal experiences. For this reason, we should be concerned that, alongside the exciting possibilities offered by these media, a deep and melancholic dissatisfaction with interpersonal relations, or a harmful sense of isolation, can also arise."

Pentagon Funds Cutting Edge Aquatic Terrain System (ATS): Pilot Program will Begin in US Pacific Command

July 24, 2015: In an exclusive interview with General Joseph Dunford, likely to be Chairman of the Joint Chiefs of Staff on 1 October 2015, he discussed the Pentagon's newest and boldest program: The Aquatic Terrain System (ATS). *"Look. With a successful ATS we could joint-operate with Black Sea Sprat and F-&^% with Russia's Black Sea Fleet. But first we have to understand the way they operate and what they want in return for working with us. It's a plus-plus situation. That same logic applies wherever there is water. Did you know that 70 percent of the Earth is water? I'm going to push Northern Command to get going with ATS with a focus on the Great Lakes and the Mississippi. The Longnose Sucker, for example, is a real force multiplier, you know. We can work with them here and in Russia. And who doesn't know about Catfish in the Mississippi? We'll get it going in Pacific Command because there is a lot of water out there and a lot of different cultures. Imagine if we had this going full steam ahead in the Indian Ocean. We'd have found that Malaysian airliner by now. There is so much good that will come out of this. We are thinking a Marine Corps three-ocean-war kind of thing, like the land base three-block-war. You know we've got to stop killing off all the marine species...We can't achieve full spectrum dominance without them."*

According to Pentagon officials, the Aquatic Terrain System has been "stood-up" with initial funding base of $70 billion. Lessons learned during the US Army's land-based Human Terrain System (LBHTS), a program valued at nearly $1 billion (deemed a stunning success by independent auditors like Horowitz, Dearing, Lee and Metz) will provide "lessons-learned, baseline, jump off points, sort of like a diving board for the ATS, so that we don't have to have catastrophic growing pains until success is created, because we saw what went on with LBHTS" said one unnamed official in SECDEF Ashton Carter's office who did not want to be quoted for this piece due to the sensitivity of the matter. When asked to clarify the statement, the Pentagon official said: "It speaks for itself."

A US Army Civil Affairs official, speaking way off the record, was asked to comment on the ATS. He stated, *"F-&^%! the ATS and F-*&^%! the LBHTS. All that F-*&^#$@! cash should have come our way. Our people could be trained to do that stuff and, besides, we've got a long history dealing with other cultures dating back to WWII. SOF doesn't need a F-*&^^% new tool, they've got it in us. We just need to be sharpened up a bit for the specific tasks. Dealing with marine life as a cultural paradigm? Are you F-^%%$ kidding me. Well, orders are orders I guess. The same kind of people that wanted to test a nuke on the moon during the Cold War are back....S-#@#! They never left. Here...Here is an image for you: All those F-&^^%$! Academics and Contractors that suck onto this thing are like those, what? Those fish that suck on sharks. WTF!!! And some of them liken themselves to Vietnam Vets! I think I'll go to Crimea!!!"*

"Think about how critical ATS is to the security of the United States," said an official with knowledge of the program who holds two PhD's and once worked in a LBHTS reach-back center in the basement of a church in Ellis, Kansas. The double-plus PhD, in an off-the-record interview, who now bills hourly to Front Page Magazine and the National Defense University, and claims he will play a key role in ATS, said in an interview conducted on a bleached picnic table on an arid, windy day in the cozy community.

"Almost 70 percent of the Earth is water. Did you know that? Thanks to LBHTS in Afghanistan and Iraq and Africa, we've got a pretty good idea about how to infiltrate groups and coerce stinky men, women and children into giving up the identities and locations of bad people. If that doesn't work we just bribe them with US dollars. Anyway, we are going to apply the same methodologies to the indigenous cultures and inhabitants of the world's oceans, lakes and rivers of the world."

According to unnamed sources in the Office of Management and Budget (OMB), the funding for ATS will also come from the National Oceanic and Space Administration (NOAA), the National Security Agency (NSA), the Central Intelligence Agency (CIA), the National Reconnaissance Office (NRO), and the newly established Clinton-Bush Foundation (CBF). "Austerity has been a real blessing for ATS," said an accountant with OMB: *"We have been able to use savings on federal programs that were used to support unemployed and impoverished Americans for ATS. I mean, that sounds kind of bad, but think about it: If we don't understand and secure the aquatic environment, those out of work and starving would lose their freedom of choice and could be killed in an attack."*

ATS has the support of members of the Research Universities Futures Consortium (RUFC) whose website states, "Collectively the universities of the Consortium have annual research expenditures of more than $11 billion which includes external grants and contracts as well as self-funded research, and educates thousands of students in all fields." A representative of one of the universities stated that of the 29 top

American research universities, all 29 are shifting their priorities to oceanography and marine biology. The anonymous representative went on: *"The next president is going to roll out the whole-of-government, whole-of-society Fish Analysis and Counter-Terrorism strategy (FACT). We will be working with our Mammalian Allies in the Ocean (MAO) to more effectively utilize the aquatic identify-kill-pacify chain (AQIKPC). We finally were able to stand-up an acronym in honor of Chairman Mao—MAO—that really defines what we are trying to do here."*

On a gray, damp, misty day aboard a NOAA vessel, rolling to and fro–and bobbing up and down–on the distressed Atlantic Ocean, a NOAA official and I sat comfortably inside the crew lounge discussing ATS. She was candid. *"Look, the Pentagon has all the cash. They are not accountable no matter how much cash goes down the tubes. And besides, there is no such thing as taxpayer money, it is all printed, fiat #$%^. NOAA will play this ATS card to get as much cash as it can. Half of our money goes to fund spy ships that track Chinese and Russian vessels. If we can get some cash to do some actual marine biology, we are all for it. There is a lot of water out here and, well, this FACT **&&^%$# may have something to it. If a Corporation can be a person, why not a Fish? They have cultures too. I'm not talking about our mammal friends we already have got them on our side. It's the coral, sharks, sting rays and even mollusks that we've got to understand."*

ATS, like LBHTS, has its detractors though they are hard to find. Even so, two academics, one from the West Coast and one from the East Coast of the United States spoke on condition of anonymity as they are employed by two of the 29 research universities identified above and feared reprisals from university administrators beholden to federal funding. The two academics are part of a structure that is viewed Horowitz, Dearing, Lee and Metz as "left wing" Marxist, communist hippies who don't like the military and, in particular, LBHTS and, now ATS.

"Come on!" said one of the academics incredulously, *"The aquatic human terrain? Lessons learned from the LBHTS? It is insane but here we are I guess. How can you argue against $70 billion? It's LBHTS all over again! And now I hear from insiders that there is a new professional association being created to siphon off pro-torture and pro-ATS, LBHTS people from the anthropology and psychological associations like APA and AAA. My sources tell me the money is going to come from the Pentagon and be funneled through the Clinton Bush Foundation. It sounds unethical but what else are non-profits for? The new association is supposedly going to be named Aquatic Land Terrain System Association. On the practical side, I guess it does make sense in terms of national security and the social sciences, and what-not."*

Asked for clarification, the other academic said, *"If you had a PhD in anthropology and done field work you'd understand exactly what I'm saying. If you haven't studied it and been there you just can't understand."*

When indicating to the academic from the East Coast that this is the same condescending argument used by the military from its God-blessed perch to brush off pesky inquiry that challenges, the academic replied, "No it isn't! And besides, who is going to listen to you, you are just some blogger."

US MILITARY'S PROGRESSIVENESS
A New Human Terrain System? Army, PACOM Séance Reveals Much

July 29, 2015: The US Army Human Terrain System (HTS) will become a "shining star, you'll see" said a music critic, part-time divinity professor, retired military officer, and former HTS contractor. He was incensed that with the alleged demise of the US Army program. It was murdered, killed and defeated, the Zombie HTS suddenly has new life thanks to *"those pro-HTS intellectuals authorized, by somebody higher up in their organizations to take up the HTS cause. Hey! Shining Star. Do you know that song by Earth, Wind and Fire?"* the former HTS contractor said. *"That should be the theme song for the new HTS ramp-up. And you know what? The HTS rebirth will be like the story of that guy from Greek mythology who was crucified, died, buried and then came back to life. What was his name, again?"*

The former contractor went on. *"Where were those people when we needed them... You know they were all hiding in the Special Operations/Low Intensity Conflict shop in the Pentagon and didn't want to go public with their support of HTS? Now they work for all kinds of contractors and think tanks and, whatever, having spun through the revolving door. Man! Can you say that anymore or do you have to say Woman too. Sorry. I got off track there. Anyway they are cashing in big-time now making as much money as they can and just waiting for the next real war—like Iraq—that involves lots of contractors, media analysts, tanks, trucks and troops. Think of the armor battles we could have with the Russians and Chinese! I miss those days"* groaned a former HTS staffer who rode along with combat hardened American soldiers who protected him while he asked questions and handed out lollipops, and other types of candy, sure to rot the teeth of the children in Afghanistan and Iraq.

An HTS staffer who works with the former HTS contractor cited earlier said this: *"You know that song by Earth, Wind and Fire, right? Shining Star is the one I am referring to like my colleague said. The lyrics that go 'You're a shining star, no matter who you are, shining bright to see, what you can truly be…That really applies to HTS because, really, it was never given a chance to be what it could truly be. But now we are seeing what it could have been thanks to articles in Foreign Policy, Bloomberg and Front Page Magazine. There will be more to come. Just wait and see."*

The woodwork has produced a flurry of pro-HTS articles ever since USA Today broke the story of its apparent demise on June 29, 2015. The most recent is in the increasingly belligerent publication Foreign Policy owned by Graham Holdings Company. The Grahams sold off the Washington Post to Jeff Bezos of Amazon fame preferring to focus on its Kaplan education and standardized testing preparation businesses. The Grahams have an interesting mix of companies engaging in health care, meeting planning (Foreign Policy), social media and combustion and lifting equipment.

What of the mysterious fate of HTS? "It is like Big Foot," said a veteran correspondent. It's true. The US Army and PACOM will not respond to media queries from anyone. Nonetheless, the demonic media, which is always at the ready to hear-out any source with verifiable information that can't be found in normal channels, is on the case with the help of US Army and PACOM insiders. *"We've conducted a number of séances with members of the media,"* said insiders. *We know that HTS still lives in pieces but will reassemble. Think of the second*

*Terminator and that liquid metal creature that is chasing
Arnold and John Conner and Conner's mom. There is a scene
in the movie where the liquid metal thing is frozen then blown
apart, its pieces are scattered all over the floor but they reunite
into the creature and it is reborn! That's HTS! And I tell you
what! HTS is going to come back like that bad-ass metal
creature."*

If that were not enough to make former HTS staffers and
proponents jump for joy, they have received significant support
from the Dentists for the Resurgence of the HTS (DRHTS)
who want to get in on the ground floor of any new HTS,
particularly since US soldiers and contractors hand out so
much candy to the conquered.

According to a DRHTS spokesperson, *"We want to get in on
the action too. There are a lot of teeth and gums in the AOR's
[area of responsibility] of the COCOMS [combatant
commands] that need fixing. We can synthesize [sic] with the
anthropologists: While they are questioning the locals, we can
be fixing their teeth and gums. I know this sounds terrible but
as we probe inside the villager's mouths we can aggressively
poke around in there causing not insignificant pain which may
yield some useful information for the HTS people. You know
kind of like that scene in the movie the Marathon Man where
Olivier, playing the Nazi dentist, abuses the cavities in
Hoffman's mouth saying, 'Is it safe.' Dentists are patriots too,"*
he added.

Alas, as Whitney Kassel of the Arkin Group laments, *"With the
quiet death of the military's controversial Human Terrain
System, America's soldiers have lost a guiding light that is
needed now more than ever."*

US MILITARY'S PROGRESSIVENESS

There is no question about that. Of course, she is right. HTS has its parallel of course. The television soap opera the Guiding Light ended in 2009, a year that saw two beginnings: The catastrophic success of HTS and the failure of the United States to murder, kill and defeat insurgents in Iraq and Afghanistan.

Am I White and Guilty of the Crime of History? No. I'm Not Going to the Reeducation Camp

August 18, 2015: *"...if you sit around and wait for the one who is in power to make up his mind that he should end it, you'll be waiting a long time. And in my opinion the young generation of whites, blacks, browns, and whatever else there is, you are living in a time when there has to be a change...a better world needs to be built...And I will join in with anyone, I don't what color he is, as long as he wants to change the miserable condition that exists on this earth."* **Malcolm X at Oxford, 1964**

"Out here in the fields. I fight for my meals. I get my back into my living. I don't need to fight to prove I'm right, I don't need to be forgiven." **Baba O'Reilly, The Who, 1971**

"And then they would have to determine how to build their suburbs on something other than human bones, how to angle their jails toward something other than a human stockyard, how to erect a democracy independent of cannibalism. I would like to tell you that such a day approaches when the people who believe them-selves to be white renounce this demon religion and begin to think of themselves as human." **Between the World and Me, Ta-Nehisi Coates, 2015**

When did my genes and "I" become guilty of thinking that they were white?

According to genetic testing results I am part of the Haplogroup R1; specifically, R1a1. Information accompanying the test results indicated that the I of Me, or the group my genes belong to, *"...appears to have arisen in the Near East or present-day Pakistan during the peak of the Ice Age about*

18,000 years ago. Until the Ice Age began to wane about 15,000 years ago, it may have been limited to the area around the Black Sea, a region that remained relatively ice-free and hospitable while much of Eurasia was covered by glaciers and tundra."

Then events transpired so that my genes "decided" they would become "white" and privileged some 12,000 years ago. *"R1 is the dominant Haplogroup in Europe today, accounting for well over half of all men. After being confined to the continent's southern fringes during the Ice Age, it expanded rapidly in the wake of the receding glaciers about 12,000 years ago. Various branches of R1 also trace the many migrations that have shaped Europe since then, from the arrival of farmers between about 10,000 and 7,000 years ago to the movements of ethnic groups such as the Anglo-Saxons and Vikings."*

I also now know that 3.0% of my DNA comes from the Neanderthal line. I know, too, that my son's mother's genes traveled, from what is now called Africa, the opposite direction from my genes, through what is now known as Asia, to what is now the West Coast of North America and, hugging the coast, made their way to Northern Brazil to the mouth of what we now call the Amazon River. Those genes which became known as Amazonian Indian merged with genes from a pool of genes from Portugal. My son's genes will likely merge with those of his wife from what we now call Trinidad by way of what is now known as India and from wherever those genes originated from.

US MILITARY'S PROGRESSIVENESS
None of this was planned.

And none of this makes any difference to those from the many bands of the human spectrum who make sure to label me White and Middle Class, just as those from other parts of the spectrum chose to tag others as Black, Asian, Pacific Islander and Latino belonging to Upper, Middle and Lower classes.

In the book Between the World and Me, Coates, I think— though I may be wrong—has said, in part, that the Species has to stop thinking it is a color, or maybe even a class, but that one must know his/her history. This made me wonder why is it that when many describe the supreme quality of a person they tend to pause and say, he or she is a 'human being'. Is this what Coates means when he says people should "think of themselves as human"? Or is he saying that being White is to be inherently evil? Or is it that Capitalism, the American Myth, and Whiteness fused into one monstrous American Democracy, with Western European origins, is destroying us all? Yet Coates seems to find solace and a sort of contradictory peace in a bastion of Western European culture now known as Paris, France.

I know my skin color is White and what that means in the most dominant economic, military and cultural power in the United States of America where roughly 17 percent are Hispanic, 12 percent Black, 4 percent Asian, 1 percent Native Americans, and 65 percent White. I do not know what it is like to be anyone else and I would not want to be like anyone else with any other history other than my own and those of my genes.

I know the history of the genocide, slavery and the rape and pillage of Blacks in Africa and America, and the destruction of the Native Peoples in north, Central and South America. I know, generally, of the ancient wars of the Pharaoh's, the Romans, the Muslims and the Greeks and the wanton slaughter and savaging of women and children in those times. I know that the slaves of the ancients were described by Varro as "speaking tools." That belief persisted in the United States for most of the country's history. I know the history of the Jewish Holocaust, the Killing Fields of Cambodia, the Rape of Nanking, Stalin and Mao's purges and executions, the human sacrifices of the Inca's, the public hangings of Blacks in America's South, the millions killed by the Belgians, and so on. I have seen what was once a human rendered into pieces.

How should I apply this knowledge?

Should I attribute the sins of the world to Whiteness? Or should I conclude that the Species itself and the dominant economic and ruling methodology of Capitalism combine to make the "demon" that Coates refers to and the "system" that Malcolm X wants us all to change: That American system, born largely of the British, Roman and Greek Systems, that relies on absurd contradictions and irony. A system that makes those from NWA and Straight Out of Compton, with all the female bashing lyrics, now part of the One Percent elite of corporate America; or the principals of the George W. Bush Administration clearly guilty of war crimes still cashing in on public office; or the poor and largely Black people that can't make $500 bail and waste away in jail; or the White miners in West Virginia killed because the mining company ignored safety rules and is found not guilty of negligence on a legal technicality; or the citizens of Detroit City denied, by a lone judge, the right to clean drinking water. And what should I make of an American society that does not care about corporate surveillance (for profit) and government monitoring of all forms of communication (to maintain security and stability for the corporations to make profits)? Where were the White Rockers, Black Rappers, and Country Music stars when the wars in Iraq and Afghanistan raged on or the beach head for the corporate and government's invasion of privacy was the home?

They, all of them, were co-opted by a political, economic and cultural system we deny every day but in which we also live, procreate, operate and profit. With all of our complaints, we don't have a functional alternative to offer. The ballot-box provides no remedy. Presidential and Congressional elections are polluted by money and interests, foreign and domestic, over which voters have no control. Politicians are bought and sold like horses prior to a race. It took a 2016 Republican presidential candidate in Donald Trump, who regularly buys and sells politicians, to acknowledge this fact. The corporate and government elite was shocked and aghast that one of their own would, well, expose Coates' "demon" so openly.

With the extremes of the American Identity Culture, social media, ubiquitous voice and audio recording, surveillance video weaving their way into all facets of American life, speech has become an action to be exercised with caution. It is an interesting coincidence that this comes on the heels of Edward Snowden's revelations of the extent of corporate and government collaboration on tracking the intimate details and movements of Americans. A poster should be made that reads, "You are to be seen but not heard and you are to speak only when spoken to. Measure your thoughts before releasing them for the record."

Fragmented, Tribal Nation

America continues its push to a more perfect Panopticon. The Atlantic Magazine reports that "A movement is arising, undirected and driven largely by students, to scrub campuses clean of words, ideas, and subjects that might cause discomfort or give offense." The World Socialists point to the dropping of Democratic Party fundraisers known formerly as Jefferson-Jackson Days. Dismissing Jackson correctly as a dumb, wealthy brut, The World Socialist's takes this view:

"Like any other historical figure, Jefferson could not catapult himself out of the times in which he lived. If he embodied more than any other leader the contradictory character of the American Revolution, which posed for the first time the claim of full human equality but had no means of establishing it, this only adds to his fascination as a historical figure. As for hypocrisy, one wonders if Wilder and Jefferson's other critics are prepared to turn over the gains they have made by speculating on the surging stock market of recent decades— money intimately bound up with the super-exploitation of the working class. Unlike Jefferson, who could say with the other revolutionists of '76 that they had staked "our lives, our Fortunes, & our sacred Honor" on a "glorious cause," Jefferson's haters in 2015 have staked absolutely nothing on their subjective and deeply a-historical attacks."

Where is American society/culture going with all this? It is certain that in this most Capitalist of societies, there will be commodification and cash to be made in the Identity Industry. The corporations have been target marketing for some time now to Blacks, Whites, Asians, Mixed, and LGBT: Fragmented markets for a fragmented nation: Just so.

Perhaps Identity Papers complete with genetic testing results are in order, or maybe public self-flagellation for those being White and therefore guilty of the woes that beset the Species and the environment. Reeducation Camps might be an option, or is college becoming the modern day reeducation camp?

Safe Spaces carried to far turn the confines of the home into that space in which people communicate with society only via the Internet and with a false identity. Nearly two million American children are being home schooled and that trend is increasing. Between corporate privatization and parental frustration with traditional 19th Century based K-12 learning modes—in both public and private schools—home schooling is on the rise.

With the religion of the mythic Judeo-Christian Gods demolished, the religion of the secular and its human gods is ascendant. Watching or reading the bombastic media and its featured commentators and guests brings the feeling of sitting in a Catholic confessional booth. "Bless me Father for I have sinned somehow and if I did not consciously sin then one of my ancestors, or my genes, did, and, in the future might."

Who will be the judges and guides in this new America that aims to be classless and colorless, and aims to reeducate all of America? It would be an extraordinary day when all Americans think that they are of no color or class, just a collection of histories and genes assembled into one United States. I'm all for it. But the history of the Species speaks against the successful implementation of such a blank slate society.

I don't think I'm White. I think I am a human being. I don't know what it is like to be rich and in the top 20 percent of money makers in the USA. I know that I'm color-labeled as White and class-labeled as Middle by the identity and false consciousness hunters that roam the American landscape.

US MILITARY'S PROGRESSIVENESS

I know I agree with Dave Chappelle, famed comedian with $10 million in the bank, who is labeled as Black and Wealthy. But I'm not a smart guy and I think that he is a human being and really funny guy with great observations of the human condition. I think that way of George Carlin, Chris Rock and the late Robin Williams. According to Chappelle: *"I support anyone's right to be who they want to be. My question is: To what extent do I have to participate in your self-image?'*

Nope, "I" don't need to be forgiven and neither do my 18,000 year-old genes.

JINSA Earns Return on Investment: 190 Americans Admirals and Generals Oppose Iran Deal

August 27, 2015: According to Carol Greenwald writing at American Thinker on 27 August 2015, Washington Post writer "[Carol] Morello does not mention how incredible it was that a few people, mostly a woman named Marsha Halteman from New Orleans, in one week could get 190 flag officers to sign a public letter stating that " *the JCPOA [Iran Deal] would threaten the national security and vital interests of the United States and, therefore, should be disapproved by the Congress.*"

Well, not so incredible at all thanks to the Jewish Institute of National Security Affairs (JINSA) very successful Generals and Admiral Program that has been in operation for many years. It has been the pipeline for 400 American military officers to visit Israel. Israel also runs similar programs for US military academy students and US law enforcement personnel.

The purpose of bringing American military personnel—and military academy students—is to maintain *"Continued and robust military-to-military dialogue between the American and Israeli defense establishments is central to JINSA's philosophy. The annual Generals and Admirals Program to Israel, in which recently retired American generals and admirals are invited to visit Israel with JINSA to meet the top echelon of the Israeli military and political leadership, ensures that the American delegation is well briefed on the security concerns of Israel, as well as the key role Israel plays as a friend and ally of the U.S. To date, JINSA has taken close to 400 retired officers to Israel, many of whom serve on JINSA's Board of Advisors."*

As of this writing the Washington Post does not appear to have updated its story on the incredible effort of Marsha Halteman who is the recipient of a prestigious award from a US combatant command.

"It gives us great pleasure to announce that JINSA's Marsha Halteman will be honored by the United States Special Operations Command (USSOCOM) with their Outstanding Civilian Service Medal for her tireless work on JINSA's Soldiers Appeal, which raises funds for military members and their families who are in need of financial assistance. Her selfless and hard work is instrumental in actively supporting a USSOCOM priority – enhancing the quality of life of the individual warrior and family. Established by the Commander of USSOCOM in September 1998, the Outstanding Civilian Service Medal recognizes civilians who have provided outstanding support or service. For Marsha, this work has been both an act of love and admiration for our men and women in uniform, as well as above and beyond the call of duty. She has truly made a difference in the lives of so many soldiers and their families and she is most deserving of this award. This prestigious award will be presented to Marsha by a senior member of the USSOCOM Command at JINSA's Spring 2014 Leadership Conference. Details of this meeting and a formal "Save the Date" will be released soon. We hope that many of you will be able to join us for the meeting and to honor Marsha."

If the US national security and political establishment had the dedication, tenacity and thoroughness of the Israeli's—in their pursuit of their national security interests, the USA would be a far more powerful country abroad and maybe at home.

Israel's interests are represented in every nook and cranny in the United States at the local, state and federal levels. They believe in Israel, nothing else. That deserves respect. American leaders, comparatively, are pathetic.

Watergate and the Washington Post's Big Lie: The Silent Coup and 40 Years of Neocon, Neoliberal War

September 22, 2015: *"The [Washington] Post lied to its readers by printing stories it knew were false, and they allowed Woodward to lie with impunity. That included printing stories that claimed that Moorer or others had never talked to us for Silent Coup, when in fact the Post's reporters not only knew they had been interviewed, but they had done so on tape. Their editors and allies waged a campaign of disinformation and intimidation against other media organizations that considered printing parts of Silent Coup or airing stories about the book."* **Len Colodny, Silent Coup**

"If you tell a lie big enough and keep repeating it, people will eventually come to believe it. The lie can be maintained only for such time as the State can shield the people from the political, economic and/or military consequences of the lie. It thus becomes vitally important for the State to use all of its powers to repress dissent, for the truth is the mortal enemy of the lie, and thus by extension, the truth is the greatest enemy of the State." **Joseph Goebbels, Minister of Propaganda, Nazi Germany**

A typical United States history text used by American public and private high school (grades 9-12) has this to say about President Richard Nixon's resignation: *"Main Idea: President Richard Nixon's involvement in the Watergate scandal forced him to resign from office. The Watergate scandal raised questions of public trust that still affect how the public and media skeptically view politicians."* **The Americans by McDougal and Littell, 2005.**

US MILITARY'S PROGRESSIVENESS

There is reference to the usual cast of characters involved with the Committee to Reelect the President and the members of the US Congress who conducted the Watergate hearings. The Wikipedia entry on Nixon and his downfall pushes the same sanitized narrative.

There is a lot of self-serving propaganda by those who cheered on the downfall of Nixon. There is lots of cheery accounts of the effectiveness of the US constitutional systems of checks and balances in which the US Congress and the judiciary rose to the challenge of the imperial presidency and set the country back on track to a corrupt-free democracy.

Nixon remains the face of political evil for many Americans. And young high school and college Americans are taught that Nixon's paranoia, insecurity, racism and disdain for all but his closest staff members were the preeminent causes for his resignation on August 9, 1974. The narratives have been sanctioned by America's political, military, academic and business elite because they are simplistic and an easy "sell" to, as Jim Morrison of the Doors once sang, a "fragile eggshell mind" which is to say, the American public.

Nixon's presidency is defined by his shortcomings and Watergate. But it really is a messy crime scene with many unsolved and unresolved matters. In this sense it remains a sort of Cold Case, desperately in need of revision to include the role of the US military Joint Chiefs of Staff and its spy operation within the National Security Council, an expose of the man who orchestrated the Watergate break-in, and the devious actions of General Alexander Haig, USA (ret.) in the National Security Council, and the dicey reporting of Bob Woodward and the Washington Post.

Len Colodny has exposed the gaps in the story in these two titles: Silent Coup: The Removal of a President (1992, re-release 2015) and The Forty Years War: The Rise and Fall of the Neocons, from Nixon to Obama (2010). The two accounts severely damage the accepted Nixon narrative. It is easy to dismiss his works as conspiracy theory if one is a disciple of the Mr. Clean theory of Watergate: All inconvenient facts are bleached from the crime scene.

But both works are impeccably written in a smooth fashion and are supported by an oil tanker's worth of interviews and references. Colodny's collected works on Nixon and Watergate are housed at Texas A&M University.

They contain "approximately 800 hours of taped interviews, with more than 100 people who were affiliated with the Nixon Administration, and those that followed. Historians, who go to Texas A&M and the online portal the University is developing, will find Colodny's extensive interviews with Nixon's closest aides and associates, including H.R. Haldeman, his Chief of Staff; Attorney General John Mitchell; and Domestic Policy Chief John Ehrlichman. It also includes exclusive interviews with "Washington Post" reporter Bob Woodward and White House Counsel John Dean, whose testimony during the 1973 Watergate Hearings helped detail Nixon's involvement in the Watergate cover-up.

Some of Colodny's key findings. are provided below. They can be accessed at Watergate.Com: Correcting the Historical Record.

US MILITARY'S PROGRESSIVENESS
On *John Dean*

"Along with showing the ties between Woodward and Haig, we also showed how Dean ordered the Watergate break-in mostly to cover his involvement with a prostitution ring run by a madam, Heidi Rikan, who was a close friend of Dean's girlfriend and wife, Maureen Biner Dean. At the time, the Deans hid behind the smoke screen that Rikan's alias, Kathie Dieter, was not Rikan. We knew that Rikan and Dieter were the same person, and we proved it. Together, the revelations provided a dramatically different version of the events that drove Nixon from office. Dean, Haig and Woodward reacted as expected; he attacked us but never landed any substantive criticisms of the book's findings."

On *Woodward and Haig*

"Bob Woodward lied to conceal his early ties to General Alexander Haig. In 1969 and 1970, Navy Lt. Bob Woodw

ard manned the Pentagon's secret communications room, which transmitted messages around the world, including the back channel communications for Henry Kissinger and President Richard Nixon. In that duty, Woodward often delivered messages from the world's top leaders to Gen. Alexander Haig, Kissinger's deputy at the National Security Council...This relationship is critical to the Watergate scandal as Haig was the key source for Woodward on his most important story, that there were deliberate erasures on a critical Nixon White House tape."

On *Deep Throat*

"Woodward, by using Throat is concealing the person that actually erased the tape or at the very least witnessed it being

erased. The word that jumps out at you is deliberate. If somebody is deliberately erasing tapes that are before Judge Sirica then we're talking about a crime."

It is significant because, if for Throat to know it was deliberate, he either erased the tape or witnessed its destruction. It is clear that both the process of elimination and Woodward's changing story about Throat as a source, that Alexander Haig is the source that told him that there were deliberate erasures on the White House tapes."

On US Military Spy Operation on Nixon-Kissinger

"During the next seven days, White House and Pentagon investigation teams sprang into action, and soon found the immediate culprit, Charles E. Radford. Radford was a career US Navy Yeoman who worked in the National Security Council offices and frequently copied classified documents and even admitted to rifling through Kissinger's briefcase.

His confession and that of his superior, Admiral Robert O. Welander, began to unravel the trail of espionage that stretched back thirteen months to November 1970. According to this historical perspective, it began when the Chairman of the Joint Chiefs of Staff, Admiral Thomas H. Moorer became suspicious of the foreign policy decisions of Nixon and National Security Advisor Henry Kissinger. These policies included how Nixon was running the war in Vietnam, his pursuit of détente with the Soviets and his plans to open up trade with China. In short, the military feared that Nixon was selling out the United States to our greatest enemies: the Communists. For this reason, a spy ring was organized inside the White House's National Security Council office for the purpose of stealing the President's most important secrets and to undermine his policies. This led to the dramatic events of December 21, 1971, the seventh day.

On that day, Nixon learned of the spy operations in all its minute details, and made a fateful decision, one that would deeply affect the course of his administration and be a factor in its demise in 1974. When told of the spy operation, Nixon initially declared it a "federal offense of the highest order." But he did not demand that anyone be prosecuted. Rather, he covered up what he learned that day, and would later re-appoint Moorer as the chairman of the Joint Chiefs.

The spy ring and his lack of reaction and retaliation would remain the deepest and most closely guarded secret of his Administration. The President even managed to conceal the presence of the spy ring during the Watergate scandal, when revealing it might well have saved his presidency. In later years he refused to acknowledge the truth about it even when confronted with the strongest available evidence — taking the secret to his grave."

Colodny's Forty Years War: Why is the USA in Such a Mess?

In 2012 I had this to say about Colodny's epic work, The Forty Year's War: He *has written an exceptionally documented and scintillating yarn of American politics dating from the World War II years to the first days of President Obama's administration. The marquee events, names and organizations common in today's political/historical analyses of those years and neocon movement and its successes and failures are all featured prominently in the book: Kissinger, Nixon, Haig, Reagan, Clinton, Bush (first and second), Obama, Rumsfeld, Cheney, Carter, Bin Laden, Paul Wolfowitz, Richard Perle, Watergate, Iran-Contra, 911, Bob Woodward, the Cold War,*

Project for a New American Century, and the American Conservative Union.

But the real power of the book comes from Colodny's digging beneath the standard American historical narrative of the panoply of events, issues and personalities of 1945-2009 to adroitly reveal the many stories of personal power grabs; political infighting between the White House/CIA, State and Defense Departments and Congress; ideological constitutional warfare; and, arguably, petty criminal activity bordering on treason. All of this is sourced with 432 "notes" to the text and a fine bibliography."

In a recent update to Silent Coup, Colodny had this to say of the findings in The Forty Years War published in 2009:

"At the time, the war in Iraq was a deadly stalemate that produced daily comparisons with Vietnam. We began investigating how the United States could become stuck in another land war without end – this time in the Middle East. Alexander Haig, the general who became Nixon's chief of staff in 1973, was the focus of some of our original research. We asked how did Haig end up working at the National Security Council for Henry Kissinger? We learned Haig had been recommended by two colleagues at the Pentagon -former Army counsel Joseph Califano and Haig's mentor Fritz G.A. Kraemer, a German-born political analyst who had also discovered *Kissinger as a young Army private during World War IL Our research showed the extent of Kraemer's influence in the military and federal government. Kraemer's hardline views shaped those of Haig, who often bridled at the policies pushed by Kissinger and Nixon. It was Haig who supplied information to the Pentagon that Nixon and Kissinger wanted to hide from the military.*

Kraemer's influence continued past Nixon into the Ford administration, where he worked with President Ford's chief of staff Donald Rumsfeld and his successor, Dick Cheney. Those two would become the Defense secretary and vice president who helped guide President George W. Bush into the disastrous invasion of Iraq. The Republican 'Peace through Strength' mantra from Ronald Reagan until this very day is based totally on Kraemer's 'Provocative Weakness Theory' The Forty Years War was published in December 2009. The book reinforced the discoveries of Silent Coup and incorporated the advances made by those influenced by Silent Coup. The findings of The Forty Years War have not been challenged..."

The American ruling class is telling Big Lies about its direct support of Nazi sympathizers instrumental in the Ukraine Coup; its attempt to dismantle Russia through sanctions, currency manipulation, and tampering with the world's oil production; its wayward children of Al Qaeda; its military encirclement of China; and its drive to cull the population of the USA through austerity programs and the creation of a militarized nation. It is all so easy to see.

Over at Fabius Maximus the results of a recent YouGov poll on a military takeover of the USA were discussed: *"Then comes the worse news. The YouGov poll shows that 29% of Americans can imagine a situation in which they would support the military seizing control of the federal government... It's an old story...the unwillingness of Rome's people to bear the burdens of self-government. Strong men contended for the throne, as seems increasingly likely to happen to America, when we turn to the police or military for succor during bad times. The people of Rome reacted to the fall of the Republic and rise of the Empire with resignation, such as*

Stoicism, Epicureanism, Hedonism, and Christianity. What philosophies or religions will we create to numb our sense of responsibility? The Founders modeled the United States after Rome, and worried that we would follow the same course. Their writings, such as the Federalist Papers, describe our love of liberty as the foundation of the Republic. The next generation or two might prove that we deserve their confidence, or not."

US MILITARY'S PROGRESSIVENESS
Vietnam 2.0 and California Dreaming in Ukraine

October 6, 2015: How involved is the US national security machinery in Ukraine? The answer to that question is contained in a sampling of information available from the US embassy in Ukraine and the Pentagon's contract awards announcements. Other publications (links provided below) have also been consulted.

Vietnam 2.0 is in the making in Ukraine. The US civil-military establishment, Republicans and Democrats alike, want a shooting war with Russia, even though it was the US that initially supported the carnage in Ukraine, not the Russians. Yet, that inconvenient reality has been nullified by the US propaganda campaign which, of course, the Russians have responded to in their own way..

Surreptitious escalation of US military involvement in Ukraine is the order of the day. Consider this comment from US Senator Jack Reid (Democrat): *"One step that should be explored, he said, is taking Ukrainian forces outside the country and training them on the provided weapon systems, "so they are ready." "Second is the possibility of transferring some of these systems from other countries into Ukraine, which doesn't raise quite the visibility of the transfer," he said. "And then there's the possibility of taking some of our systems and beginning to...deploy them to training areas particularly so that they can train on them and have them ready to move into areas of conflict," he said... He also said Ukraine has an extensive military industrial base that could be used to produce the weapons, but that would take time and financing."*

It's becoming apparent that the US Army, US Air Force and US Navy want, respectively, the 21st Century versions of the

Battle of Prokhorovka, Hiroshima/Nagasaki, and the Battle of Midway. Maybe the plan is to make proxy wars so hot that world war will follow with Russia (and China). It's doubtful that the US Marines want another Iwo Jima or that US special operations warfighters want to be dropped into no-win situations (they are smarter than that).

No matter, Americans shoot up war like a junkie shoots up heroin. Destroying Syria and Iraq as functioning states did not provide the high, nor did the War on Terror, or the War on Drugs, or Afghanistan (10,000 US soldiers remain there). The next score needs to be higher-dose, longer lasting, "real man, you know what I'm saying."

US-Ukraine Cooperation, Deals

California–Ukraine State Partnership Program (US Embassy, Ukraine): SPP Mission is to promote democracy, free market economies and military reform, by establishing long-term institutional affiliations and personal relationships at the state and local level. The California – Ukraine partnership directly supports both the goals of the US Ambassador to Ukraine and Commander, U.S. European Command. As part of the Governor's Cabinet, the Adjutant General of the California National Guard facilitates partnerships throughout the state and local governments in California as well as the private sector. Recently, a tuberculosis clinic in Odessa was renovated with funds provided by this office

Defense Cooperation between US and Ukraine (US Embassy, Ukraine): Joint Contact Team Program-Ukraine (JCTP). The mission of the Joint Contact Team Program (JCTP) is to deploy US military teams to Ukraine to acquaint the Ukrainian military with various aspects of western militaries. The program was developed in 1992 to assist the armed forces of Ukraine, as the military of one of the emerging democracies of Central and Eastern Europe.

International Military Education and Training (IMET, US Embassy, Ukraine): The IMET Program provides training in the United States to selected foreign military and related civilian personnel. The overarching security cooperation objective is to promote stability, democratization, military professionalism, and closer relationships with NATO.

Foreign Military Sales/Foreign Military Financing (US Embassy, Ukraine): The FMF program assists the Ukrainian military in conducting defense reform by providing funds for Ukraine to purchase US military equipment and services.

Defense Contracts for Ukraine (Pentagon Website):
September 2015: Aerovironment Inc., Monrovia, California, was awarded a $9,049,306 firm-fixed-price foreign military sales contract (Ukraine) for the small UAV RQ-11B Raven analogy system. Work will be performed in Monrovia, California, with an estimated completion date of May 11, 2016. One bid was solicited with one received. Fiscal 2010 other procurement funds in the amount of $9,049,306 were obligated at the time of the award. Army Contracting Command, Natick, Massachusetts, is the contracting activity (W911QY-15-C-0102).

September 2015: Harris Corp., Rochester, New York, was awarded a $65,669,054 firm-fixed-price, incrementally funded foreign military sales contract (Ukraine, Lithuania, Lebanon, Chad, Niger, Mauritania, Kenya, Somalia, Uganda, Ethiopia) with options for Harris Radio Systems, (multiband (AN/PRC-152A: AN/PRC-117G), high frequency (HF) and dismount), antennas, BMS software, data terminals, touch tablets, field service representatives, and training for installation, operation and maintenance. Work will be performed in Rochester, New York, with an estimated completion date of Sept. 30, 2016. One bid was solicited with one received. Fiscal 2015 operations and maintenance funds in the amount of $38,950,534 were obligated at the time of the award. Army Contracting Command, Aberdeen, Maryland, is the contracting activity (W91CRB-15-C-5029).

July 2015: AM General, South Bend, Indiana was awarded a $372,936,476 firm-fixed-price multi-year foreign military sales contract (Afghanistan, Iraq, Kenya, Lebanon, Ukraine, Tunisia) with options for 2,082 High Mobility Multipurpose Wheeled Vehicles (HMMWVs) and contractor unique spare parts. Work will be performed in Mishawaka, Indiana with an estimated completion date of April 29, 2016. Bids were solicited via the internet with one received. Fiscal 2015 other procurement funds in the amount of $372,936,476 were obligated at the time of the award. Army Contracting Command is the contracting activity (W56HZV-15-C-0155).

Training the Ukrainian Military

July 2015 (from Defense Industry Daily): Ukraine will receive external link an additional $500 million from the US government to finance the training of Ukrainian military personnel. The Obama administration modestly increased US training to include Defense Ministry forces in June external link, after US personnel were first deployed to train Interior Ministry troops in April. The announcement comes several days after a report external link published by the Center for New American Security identified several strategic deficiencies with US policy on defense assistance.

US MILITARY'S PROGRESSIVENESS
Propaganda Generates Profits: Bellicose Neighbor = Joint Procurement

The Baltic states of Estonia, Latvia and Lithuania are discussing external link the possibility of collaborative defense procurement. The NATO states border an increasingly belligerent Russia and may also seek to join the development activities of the Nordic Defense Cooperation's external link (NORDEFCO) Military Cooperation Areas in a bid to maximize rising defense investment. Estonia already meets NATO's target defense spend of 2% GDP, with Latvia and Lithuania planning to meet this target by 2020. Lower per-unit costs through larger equipment buys are likely to drive joint investment, with air defense systems specifically mentioned. The US and Poland have been keen to develop the Baltics' air defense systems, with Sweden also planning a revamp of its capabilities.

The Neoliberal Engineering of Gender and Social Acceptance

November 6, 2015: *"The modification of gender from being a variable of sex to an independent cultural order of knowledge entailed a shift in the intelligibility and governability of sexual lives, bodies and selves. By defining it as explicitly separated from sex with its own series of data, Robert J. Stoller introduced gender as a phenomenon with its own constituent parts (gender, gender role, gender identity) and formative mechanisms that needed to be discovered, examined and exploited to cure, placate and normalize sexual deviancy. In the process it was a mechanism not only of psychiatric power but also of disciplinary power and biopower, pathologizing minds and normalizing bodies to fit the reproductive imperatives of postwar US capitalism."*

Gender equality policy operates as a biopolitical mechanism for raising and optimizing below level fertility rates and promoting the industriousness of the population. Gender equality policy has therefore been formulated to accommodate aims that are both biopolitical and bioeconomic, that is, the capitalization of vitality in liberal capitalist societies. The political deployment of gender provides biopower with new access to an array of social relations, multiplying and optimizing the reach and utility of biopower in society. The accompanying attempt to induce female subjects to make choices that allow them to free themselves from the antiquated baggage of gender roles to both produce the species and create capital only makes sense in the context of neoliberal governmentality. **Jemima Repo, The Biopolitics of Gender (Oxford, 2016)**

US MILITARY'S PROGRESSIVENESS
Live Stock

Culturally engineered humans are being produced to meet the
design specifications of the neoliberal, capitalist system. Those
specifications call for the production of psychologically
modified individuals to view human and non-human life like
the stock that is traded on Japan's Nikkei or the New York
Stock Exchange. Concepts such as emotion, gender, ethics,
morals, sex, religion, living, dying, war, soul, spirit or work are
relevant only in as much as they have value to capital. More
importantly, such individuals must be made to believe that their
worth, and meaning in the universal scheme of things, is as
human capital, as living tradable stock, nothing more.

Perhaps within 200 years, more or less, the neoliberal capitalist
system will create a reality in which some sort of intelligent
human machine life will rapidly reproduce itself and come to
dominate what will be considered to be legacy models of
culturally engineered and genetically altered humanity.
Naturally, the latter will be phased out and, perhaps, used to
create new biological parts for the new models. Whatever
beliefs systems exist then will likely have their origins in the
neoliberal capitalist system in which value, buying and selling,
costs and benefits, and return on investment are the equivalent
of the Ten Commandments.

There should not be any hue and cry over this likely future. Are
not we already programmable creatures? Television, cinema
and computer screens are packed with science fiction
programming that depicts the merging of human and non-
human life with machines. A perpetual war on terror
undertaken by the USA has provided the opportunity for
science, engineering, computing and medicine to build
prototype human machines. World War II and the Cold War

produced a stunning array of scientific and technological movement (we can't say conclusively that it was advancement). What will World War III produce? Somewhere in the backrooms and thinks tanks of the world's most powerful countries, that cost/benefit calculus has been done.

The use of conservative or liberal tradition, morality, religion (let's include art too) for the psychological and demographic control by the world's elite has fallen into disfavor. The next generation tools for such whipsawing are far more subtle and effective and have been or are being created by the new wizards of the day: Computer Scientists, Psycho-pharmacologists, Financiers, Venture Capitalists, Social Scientists, Physical and Biological Scientists, Geneticists and Cognitive Neuroscientists, among others. These grand brains, brilliant in their respective fields, exist largely on the dole thanks to the good graces of neoliberal capitalist taskmasters who have the wealth to fund research or steer funding to one program over another.

The key questions for the neoliberal capitalist financiers/funders concern costs, benefits, return on investment, profitability and marketability. On a grander scale, those same questions apply to war-making (Bush II and Iraq II), government overthrows (Obama and Ukraine), currency manipulation (Western financiers and Russia), who eats and who doesn't (Capital's imposition of austerity), or which masses of people can be culled or sacrificed (Syrians, Iraqi's, Palestinians, American Blacks, Native Americans, etc.). But what about wealthy politicians, lobbyists, academia and dedicated military commanders dedicated to uphold the US Constitution? They are pawns within the neoliberal capitalist system serving either as errand boys or muscle for their masters. If they serve well, they are rewarded with a relative modicum of wealth like US politicians Bill and Hillary Clinton. The US general's payoff is a quick turn through the revolving door into the board rooms of defense corporations or venture capital firms.

Show Me the Money!

The 1 percenters in the USA view the 99 percent as peasants scurrying about to make ends meet, worrying about paying the bills, rushing to get home to sit down and watch television or play video games, and praying to the Capitalist Gods to ensure the health and welfare of the children; who, by the way, are little more than consumer durables in Human Capital Theory and, it would seem to marketers, in practice.

According to Becker: *"The theory of the demand for consumer durables is a useful framework in analyzing the demand for children. As consumer durables, children are assumed to provide "utility." The utility from children is compared with that from other goods. In principle the net cost of children can be easily computed...Children are viewed as a durable good, primarily a consumer's durable, which yields income, primarily psychic income, to parents. Fertility is determined by income, child costs, knowledge, uncertainty, and tastes. An increase in income and a decline in price would increase the demand for children, although it is necessary to distinguish between the quantity and quality of children demanded. The quality of children is directly related to the amount spent on them..."*

The beauty of the neoliberal capitalist order is its ability to liquidate or create, belief systems for the sake of creating virtual and real value, and profit. The neoliberal capitalist system, in this sense, is "just" and "nondiscriminatory." Take, for example, the gender equity movement, the legitimization/legalization of LGBT lifestyles, diversity campaigns in schools and offices, and the women's movement.

The dollar, yen, ruble or British pound abhor limitations on their ability to exponentially reproduce. Prejudicial regulations that limit the amount of labor value that can be exploited for profit are senseless in the neoliberal capitalist model. All must work and all must "be" value and create more value for the system. Belief systems that keep someone in the home to take care of the kids are now antithetical to the prevailing order. The spouse/partner should be in agreement that the children should go to the day care center. The day care center relies on two working couple households to keep the center operational and as a place of employment for locals. The neoliberal imperative coerces the couple into work not only for basic life security needs, but because by working more the couple ostensibly earns more to spend on its offspring and in the economy at large (not to mention the profit they enable their employer to turn).

Heterosexuality: So Lame

According to Experian, gay males make more money than heterosexuals. From an economic perspective, this is real value, even stability. *"...gay males actually have higher discretionary spending per capita than heterosexual men. In fact, gay men live in households that devote $6,794 per capita annually to nonessentials, which is $753 more than what heterosexual men spend. Specifically, the average household income of a partnered gay man is $115,500 versus $102,100 for a heterosexual married/partnered man...36% of LGBT adults today are aged 18 to 34 versus 26% of the heterosexual population in that age range."*

US MILITARY'S PROGRESSIVENESS

The non-believing 'atheist' in the neoliberal capitalist world is arguably someone like Pope Francis who lives and acts humbly washing the feet of the poor and seeks to mend the world not destroy it. To the ruthless financiers or currency manipulators, despicable politicians, Ivory Tower academics Compassion and empathy matter only in as much as they can be used to generate value and profit.

From the perspective of the neoliberal capitalists, The Pope's exhortation before the US Congress to limit the activities of the world's arms sellers/merchants of death was an outrage. After all, the benefits of arming allies and dictatorial powers include: reduction of populations with limited disposable income; profits associated with replacement of used/dated weaponry; acquisition of territory; technology transfer from battlefield to local law enforcement, and so on.

The sooner the old school belief system that the Pope represents can be dumped, the better according to the capitalists; after all, markets must be created for Capitalism to survive. Even Identity can be sold. For example, the LGBT market is valued at approximately $800 billion. Who in their right mind would ignore the money making opportunities in that burgeoning market? And besides, there is the matter of the neoliberal capitalist system's need to maintain an appropriate fertility rate. If straight men and women aren't doing the job in the reproductive arena then someone has to mind the store. Productive economies depend on new crops of children. According to Steve Roth, Principal of OutThinkPartners, in a presentation titled Targeting a Dream Market, "More gay men and lesbians are having babies." IN the not too distant future, same sex couples will have their own genetically minted kids.

US MILITARY'S PROGRESSIVENESS

Writing in the March 18, 2015 issue of Time Magazine, Dr. Guy Ringler notes:

"There likely will be a time when reproductive science could create an embryo from the cells of two men or two women... Stem cell research has demonstrated that human skin cells and fibroblasts (a different kind of adult cell) can be turned into embryonic stem cells. Now, researchers at Cambridge University and the Weizmann Institute of Science in Israel have shown that embryonic stem cells can be programmed to form primordial germ cells. These are the stem cells that can go on to form either eggs or sperm. If scientists can figure out how to turn a primordial germ cell that originated from the skin of a man into an egg, could it be fertilized with his partner's sperm? Research using primordial germ cells in mice has shown that these cells can be turned into eggs and sperm capable of forming pups (baby mice). Many experiments were required, but tremendous knowledge was gained.

Just like straight couples, many gay men and lesbians are eager to have a genetic relationship with their children. At times, I've taken sperm from one gay man and matched it with the eggs of his partner's sister to create a stronger genetic bond between the couple and their child. But these new scientific developments could bring that process full-circle."

So you say marriage should be confined to a union between a biological man and biological woman. You say that the children—whether adopted, surrogate birthed, test tube, or genetically created—will suffer at the hands two same sex parents? That is incorrect.

According to the American Pediatrics Association: *"Many studies have assessed the developmental and psychosocial outcomes of children whose parents are gay or lesbian and note that a family's social and economic resources and the strength of the relationships among members of the family are far more important variables than parental gender or sexual orientation in affecting children's development and well-being... Because marriage strengthens families; and, in so doing, benefits children's development, children should not be deprived of the opportunity for their parents to be married. Paths to parenthood that include assisted reproductive techniques, adoption, and foster parenting should focus on competency of the parents rather than their sexual orientation... Thirty-one percent of same-gender couples who identified as spouses and 14% of those who identified as unmarried partners indicated that they were raising children, more than 111000 in all. In addition to these parents, many single gay men and lesbians are also raising children. Combined, current estimates suggest that almost 2 million children younger than 18 years are being raised by at least 1 gay or lesbian parent in the United States"*

The reproductive imperatives of the 21st Century have been engineered in accordance with the demands of the neoliberal capitalist model. Was there any other way to get to there?

What an incredible waste of time it was kowtowing to those moralities, ethics, religions and codes of social conduct from yesteryear. There's nowhere to go on this planet to escape the globalized neoliberal capitalist system or its influence. We all live or die in it. As the Outlaw Josie Wales said to Ten Bears:

Ten Bears: *You are the grey rider. You would not make peace with the Bluecoats. You may go in peace.*

Josie Wales: *I reckon not. I got no place else to go.*

US MILITARY'S PROGRESSIVENESS

Ten Bears: *Then you will die.*

Josie Wales: *I came here to die with you--or to live with you.*

Daesh is a Global Insurgency, Not a Terrorist Group: Structural Changes Needed to Counter ISIS-ISIL

November 16, 2015: The system is broken. Governments and state institutions are increasingly incapable of protecting their own civilians from militants who have become weary of seeing their homelands, friends, relatives, children, livelihoods, futures and institutions obliterated. They are sick of the oppression of their own Western backed governments to the point that death is no longer relevant to them.

Until structural cracks in the foundation of the global capitalist system are addressed and repaired, the rewind button will stay locked and organizations like Daesh-ISIS-ISIL-AQ, and ultimately its offshoots, will continue to kill and maim citizens with impunity. They have seen the same done to their own, so why should they spare anyone else?

As long as the global economy continues to make surviving from paycheck to paycheck a reality for the bulk of the Earth's populace, the more destabilized societies will become, and the more Daesh or other radical groups will be able to recruit from the outcasts. The rise of Donald Trump in the United States, Le Pen in France, and the neo-Nazi's in Ukraine are foreboding signs. Austerity measures are a force multiplier for Daesh. Internal warfare can no longer be confined with borders.

The Internet and World Wide Web and social media are continuing to diminish the role of the State which can only confront challenges in a binary format of military action or economic sanctions. Insurgent groups like Daesh continue to exercise media and technological prowess that its opponents can't match.

US MILITARY'S PROGRESSIVENESS

How effective has the United States' (other nations too) political-military-intelligence strategy and tactics been in countering Daesh-AQ insurgencies? Let the events of 911 be a starting point going forward in time. What does the record show? Have insurgents been contained in their homelands? Is fighting them there really working? What's Daesh-ISIL-ISIS-AQ been up to since they have felt the full fury of American and European military might in Iraq and Afghanistan, punitive air strikes in Syria and the overthrow of Gaddafi in Libya?

Dial M for Murder

Daesh/AQ notches kills and maims in France (Paris), Russia (Metrojet 9268 in Egypt), Southern Lebanon, Turkey (Ankara), Syria, Iraq, Afghanistan, Sudan/South Sudan, Libya, Yemen, USA (9-11), Spain (Madrid Subway), and England (7/7).

According to Scott Atron writing in the Guardian: *"Radical Arab Sunni revivalism, which Isis now spearheads, is a dynamic, revolutionary countercultural movement of world historic proportions, with the largest and most diverse volunteer fighting force since the Second World War. In less than two years, it has created a dominion over hundreds of thousands of square kilometers and millions of people. Despite being attacked on all sides by internal and external foes, it has not been degraded to any appreciable degree, while rooting ever stronger in areas it controls and expanding its influence in deepening pockets throughout Eurasia.*

Simply treating Isis as a form of "terrorism" or "violent extremism" masks the menace. Merely dismissing it as "nihilistic" reflects a willful and dangerous avoidance of trying to comprehend, and deal with its profoundly alluring amoral mission to change and save the world. And the constant refrain that Isis seeks to turn back history to the Middle Ages is no more compelling than a claim that the Tea Party movement wants everything the way it was in 1776. The truth is more complicated.

As Abu Mousa, Isis's press officer in Raqqa put it: *"We are not sending people back to the time of the carrier pigeon. On the contrary, we will benefit from development. But in a way that doesn't contradict the religion.We must work to expose the weakness of America's centralized power by pushing it to abandon the media psychological war and the war by proxy until it fights directly.. We must capture the rebelliousness of youth, their energy and idealism, and their readiness for self-sacrifice, while fools preach 'moderation' (wasatiyyah), security and avoidance of risk."*

Let's Destabilize Everything

How many civilian deaths has the West, led in war or supported by the USA, caused in Iraq, Syria, Afghanistan, Sudan, West Bank, Gaza, Libya, Somalia or Yemen? How many displaced persons/refugees/migrants have the Western led wars created? The European Union, France in particular, now know how foolish the destruction of Afghanistan, Syria, Iraq and Libya were. So do Lebanon, Jordan, and Iran who are home to many thousands of displaced persons escaping from the fallout of maniacal military adventures. Daesh war planners must be thrilled that their personnel had such a fluid pipeline into the heartlands of the "crusaders" in Europe.

The Daesh-AQ vs. The World conflict has at least a dozen causes dating back to the fomenting of radical Islam by the United States and Saudi Arabia for the purposes of destroying

the USSR (starting in Afghanistan). One could even point, as
Daesh did early on in its ascendancy, to Sykes Picot.

So, lets fast forward to 2015.

The talent pool for Daesh to recruit from is wide, deep, young
and unemployed with few prospects. The global unemployment
rates for those 14-24 year old global population are
dangerously high. Consider these figures for youth out of work:
France, 24 percent; Greece, 58 percent; Iraq, 34 percent;
Lebanon, 20 percent; Libya, 51 percent; Saudi Arabia, 27
percent; Spain, 57 percent; Sudan, 24 percent; Tunisia, 31
percent; UK, 20 percent; Syria, 30 percent; Yemen, 30 percent
and the United States, 16 percent. Many of these human
"percentages" have known nothing but war and carnage, and
recognize that their efforts during the "Arab Spring" were
futile; for example, a 2013 coup—supported by the United
States and Saudi Arabia–negated the open elections that put
Mohamed Morsi into office.

World political, military, economic and academic leaders are of
a mind that punishing military action, domestic repression,
economic sanctions, media bombast, and torture will ultimately
eliminate groups like Daesh. The thinking is that fear as a tool
of control or oppression still matters. It's the same kind of
thinking that drives the grand brains in the United States to
reignite a Cold War with China and Russia, engaging in
brinkmanship right up to the borders of those two countries
emplacing missile defense systems or engaging in pissing
contest flybys using nuclear weapons carrying platforms like
the B-52.

US MILITARY'S PROGRESSIVENESS
Learning from Daesh

Is the Western World following the Daesh-AQ playbook? According to Atron: *"There is a playbook, a manifesto: The Management of Savagery/Chaos, a tract written more than a decade ago under the name Abu Bakr Naji, for the Mesopotamian wing of al-Qaida that would become Isis. Think of the horror of Paris and then consider these, its principal axioms...Hit soft targets...Diversify and widen the vexation strikes against the crusader-Zionist enemy in every place in the Islamic world, and even outside of it if possible, so as to disperse the efforts of the alliance of the enemy and thus drain it to the greatest extent possible."*

It conscientiously exploits the disheartening dynamic between the rise of radical Islamism and the revival of the xenophobic ethno-nationalist movements that are beginning to seriously undermine the middle class – the mainstay of stability and democracy – in Europe in ways reminiscent of the hatchet job that the communists and fascists did on European democracy in the 1920s and 30s. The fact that Europe's reproductive rate is 1.4 children per couple, and so there needs to be considerable immigration to maintain a productive workforce that can sustain the middle class standard of living, is a godsend for Isis, because at the same time there has never been less tolerance for immigration. Therein lies the sort of chaos that Isis is well positioned to exploit."

In the United States, trillions of dollars have been expended to, ostensibly, protect Americans at home and abroad. But in the process, since the post-WWII years, the United States federal government has been responsible—through ill-advised military adventures, coups or sheer ignorance—for the deaths and wounding of many millions of civilians in other countries. The

United States has not produced a Stalin or Mao yet, but as the years pass, the body count in terms of the dead, wounded and displaced mounts at home and abroad.

Ill-conceived United States military adventures abroad, or blind support for countries like Saudi Arabia and Egypt, will increasingly cause problems for the organizations that, in fact, really do protect and defend Americans: Law enforcement personnel, fire fighters, emergency medical personnel, and covert special operations forces, etc. These individuals and organizations work within a warlike American landscape in which approximately 14,000 Americans are murdered and 79,000 raped each year.

And the odds of getting away with a crime in the United States are not that bad. According to the FBI: "When considering clearances of violent crimes, 64.1 percent of murder offenses, 40.6 percent of rape offenses (revised definition), 40.0 percent of rape offenses (legacy definition), 29.4 percent of robbery offenses, and 57.7 percent of aggravated assault offenses were cleared." If translated another way, there is a 36 percent chance of getting away with murder, and a nearly 60 percent chance of raping someone without consequence.

One can't help but recognize that America's propensity for violence in everything from video games to the militarization of sports like football is pathological, even infecting policies like federal funding for the unemployed and impoverished and segments of the populations that would sooner send immigrants from Central and South America to Guantanamo Bay.

How violent is American society? According to an unflinching report by the World Socialist website:

US MILITARY'S PROGRESSIVENESS

"The United States incarcerates children at a rate that far surpasses the rest of the world. According to the Equal Justice Initiative, almost 3,000 children have been convicted and given life sentences without the chance of parole. On any given day, 10,000 children are held captive in adult jails and prisons, where they face high chances of sexual assault. Tens of thousands more are held in juvenile centers that are so commonplace they are called by their nickname, juvies.

Protection Racket

So what is this protection racket all about? What does it mean to protect citizens? What are they being protected from? Should protection mean the State ensures, even enforces, a robust mixed economy that can employ nearly all of its citizens, provides health insurance, and that favors all and not just a few, thereby eliminating much of "life's" intolerable uncertainties? Would protection include forcing corporations and financiers to stay home and pay their share of taxes?

Who can't sympathize for those killed, wounded or grieving on either side of this conflict? I certainly do. One moment rocking out with a heavy metal band in Paris and in the next instant a bullet in your stomach and you're bleeding out on the floor. But should I not value the suffering of those in Afghan wedding parties, MSF in Kunduz, children slaughtered/starved in Iraq, Christian communities decimated or forced to migrate (Iraq-Syria), Sunni and Shia conflict enflamed by religious zealots and Western leaders? The human being no longer matters in this world.

Former Secretary of Defense Donald Rumsfeld once said that people are fungible. He was vilified for this by me, among others. But he was right. This philosophy is at the core of human capital theory and the globalized capitalist system that the United States created and that now operates in various guises in China, Russia, India, Brazil, and in every country on the planet except North Korea.

A system that assigns use value to life has no place for the sanctity of life.

In the end, the United States, the European Union and Russia will conduct a large scale ground invasion of Syria and portions of Iraq. They will divvy up the spoils probably along the lines of Sykes Picot, and throw some of the carcass Turkey and Iran's way. It'll be like a sectored Berlin post WWII.

The war will not end though. Daesh has spread all over the globe. They know well that their home bases in Syria and Iraq will be destroyed. When the anti-Daesh forces (ground troops, mercenaries, embedded media) show up in Daesh strongholds will they even be there? How far will the chase for Daesh go on? Will it extend into every continent on Earth? What about their affiliates in Saudi Arabia, Egypt, Afghanistan, and Pakistan, or maybe right here at home?

On this point there is certainty: Security will continue to override liberty and freedom of expression. Dissent will be a perilous act. Rehearse the singing of your nation's national anthem and practice your nation's pledge of allegiance. Don't fasten your seatbelt for the bumpy night as the actress Betty Davis once said. Rather, be prepared to move and adapt quickly.

The Emerging Dystopian Republic: Systems Engineering the Human from Birth thru Death

January 16, 2016: The systems engineering discipline is at once an exceptional holistic and precision tool for conceptualizing, designing, fielding, maintaining, upgrading and recycling systems as diverse as handheld mobile communications devices, the Internet/WWW, urban transport systems, and US military weapons systems like the Ford-Class aircraft carrier. Generally speaking, the systems engineering methodology considers the entire life cycle of the system/product from beginning to end. The life cycle process must account for other key inputs: materials, human/humans, labor, time, funding, costs/prices, operational environment, disposal, etc.

A critical determinant in the overall systems engineering process is often the role of human capital: Where does the human fit into the system? What kind of human can the system tolerate? How much will it cost to integrate the human into the system? What will it cost to train the human to function within or with a complex system? Is the human necessary to the functioning of the system? Where are system-friendly humans to be found?

The systems engineering discipline's holistic tool must be employed to look beyond the large-scale system, machine or mega-city, that can be constructed, maintained and managed, and answer another set of pertinent questions. What is the system of culture, politics, and economy—the totality—in which complex communications networks, machines, mega-cities, nuclear weapons, militaries, political parties, rules/regulations, and people, places and things, etc., operate and exist? And what are the characteristics of the system in its totality that engenders the development of new subsystems within that larger system? What endogenous and exogenous influences prompt the system in totality or its subsystems to engage in constructive and/or destructive activity?

Survival of the System

Here in the United States there is a significant convergence of events that together are catalyzing the development of a future dystopian, deterministic republic. The survival of this system—and its primary mission to retain unmatched global military and economic dominance–will depend largely on channeling individuals, and clusters of individuals, into life-slots to meet the system's needs, not individual aspirations based on some mythical American dream (which, like the Gods of old, will eventually fade away). Individuals/groups will be subjected to life-long genetic testing, health monitoring and performance based measurements of effectiveness at study, work or play.

They will be engineered to support the system.

The engineering of human systems will begin with the cultivation, testing and monitoring of male and female genomic material, the fetus in test tube, utero or incubator, and on through formal educational stages (college only for the few) continuing into the workplace, retirement and even death (what is the cheapest way to die and dispose of the body?). In short, individuals/groups life cycles will be subjected to necessarily intrusive systems engineering practices. The dystopian, deterministic republic's survival and mission success will depend on the discipline of systems engineering and the discipline of acceptance by individuals/groups. Educating individuals/groups to the design and purpose of the dystopian, deterministic republic is essential, but more on that later.

Such statements conjure up any number of texts in science fiction and film: We, 1984, Brave New World, Clockwork Orange, Soylent Green, Blade Runner, GATTACA and hundreds more. The dystopian, deterministic republic may contain elements of the authors/directors notions of dystopian society as portrayed in their works but, at the moment, it's difficult to envision any salvation for humanity through fantastical computing technologies and medical breakthroughs. Indeed, as Nick Bostrom points out in his book Superintelligence, when the machines become aware and intelligent, they are likely to do away with humanity.

There are dozens of visible currents leading to a unique convergence which will ignite the rapid development of the dystopian, deterministic republic. Three currents are listed below but are in no particular order, though they are all interconnected with synergies between each. They exist, like all things under the American sun, within the universe of neoliberal capitalism which uses people, places and things, to include the US Constitution, to advance the interests of those with the power and wealth to manipulate, if not the total system, then large subsystems within it. One example is the currency speculation of George Soros who "broke the Bank of England."

Three Currents

The first is the Internet/WWW of Things and People or, in clearer terms, Ubiquitous Intelligent Machine and Human Sensors located in globalized public and private space. Machines and humans record, store and share activity which is surveilled, tracked and shared by the autonomous tracking machinery of government and commercial enterprises. Adult humans willingly provide non-Internet data that will be their children's undoing. For example, US federal, local and state governments fund the operation of P-20 education data collection and database development based on measures of performance and, in some cases, medical data. From pre-school to 20 years of age, this data is collected and tracked and shared with post-secondary education institutions, policy planners, corporations/businesses, think tanks, polling groups, and the National Security apparatus. Beyond the obvious uses, the data is used, in some cases, for educational intelligence used to predict what student/students are at risk and, of course, who or what is putting them at risk (teachers, parents, neighbors, organization, etc.).

The second is Plutocratic Dominance of Political and Economic Power Centers. Robert Reich's book Saving Capitalism (2015) documents the overrunning of what he calls the five building blocks of capitalism and democracy by the wealthy and powerful. This results in the damming of channels through which 70 percent of Americans used to wield "countervailing power". According to Reich, the five building blocks of capitalism are *"Property (what can be owned); Monopoly (what degree of market power is permissible), Contract (what can be bought and sold, and on what terms); Bankruptcy (what happens when purchasers can't pay up); and Enforcement (how to make sure no one cheats on any of these rules)."*

Each of the five blocks is largely dominated by individuals and organizations who have access to funds that can be used to lobby and litigate for their own business interests. Examples include keeping wages stagnant, raiding pension funds, privatizing public education, lax antitrust enforcement, buying politicians through cash contributions, waging protracted litigation as a cost of doing business, union busting, etc.

Plutocrats seek the roll back of New Deal and Great Society programs, and any modern versions of them (food stamps, unemployment compensation, Social Security/Medicare, etc.).

The *third* is the De-Sovereignitization of Household and National Boundaries by US political, military and economic leaders. This means, for Americans, the elimination of the Fourth Amendment to the US Constitution. In like manner, American political and military leaders have unilaterally erased long standing borders between nations and blatantly ignore the quaint notions of international law. This is openly stated by President Obama in his national security strategies and speeches. President Obama, like all of his predecessors, has indicated that the US will advance its interests regardless of the entreaties or actions of other nations. If there is such a thing as a Fourth Amendment in international law that other nations feel they have codified to thwart US intrusions into their societies, homes and communications, they are badly mistaken.

Looney Tunes Country

The US has been on a global rampage since 911 like the Tasmanian devil portrayed in the cartoon series Looney Tunes. The "Americans are coming" strikes fear and loathing around the globe. There is a difference between the activities of the US government and international corporations in the 21st Century and the 20th Century's Cold War. During the latter conflict the USA felt compelled to keep its involvement in the overthrow of governments in Central and South America, Iran, Italy, Congo, etc., classified and quiet.

But now such activity is in-your-face, publicized and supported by mainstream media outlets. Ukraine, Syria, Iraq, Libya and Yemen come to mind as direct and overt military/intelligence operations promoted publicly through the fusion of military information support operations and civilian strategic communications that affected and distorted civilian media reportage and, hence, the American public's perceptions of the geopolitical dynamics involved and at risk. Since the US Congress and Supreme Court are largely ignorant of the complexities involved in such matters, they are no different that the masses in the general public. It's worth mentioning that the past decade has been the deadliest for journalists in terms of killings and the elimination of foreign and domestic reporters/editors through layoffs.

Leaders in the USA have stood around idly, smiling even, as Bahrain and Egypt brutalized protestors there seeking basic human rights. Indeed, the similarities between those events and the shooting deaths of Black teenagers by rogue law enforcement personnel in Missouri, Maryland, Ohio, New York, etc., is typically met with an "oh, well" by American leadership. The elite's thinking goes something like this: What's 16,000 Americans murdered each year, millions of American children and adults in poverty, millions more unemployed or under employed, the destruction of the middle class, income disparity, crumbling infrastructure, and hundreds of thousands of military veterans suffering have to do with me?

Americans roam the planet via unmanned aerial vehicles and special forces in search of rag-tag groupings of "terrorists" and maniacal drug lords who are deemed existential security threats to a country, the USA, with a $17 trillion GDP a year economy and a domestic and national security apparatus (law enforcement, homeland security included, overseas military operations, intelligence activities, etc.) that easily absorbs $3 trillion of that GDP each year. It is a bargain, really.

Americans are ruled by a collective of Vilos Cohagen's from the movie Total Recall (original). Upon being informed that the oxygen cutoff he approved to punish mutant workers will cause them all to die, Cohagen responds, "Fuck 'em," just so.

So where, exactly, do the grand brains that rule begin to re-engineer a society to accept administered, deterministic freedom and life (see Herbert Marcuse's work *One Dimensional Man for details*)? Look no further than America's public education system. K-16 public education is being ripped apart and privatized by hedge fund managers, ongoing economic recession, charter school supporters, income segregation and austerity. In fact, income disparity is linked to education disparity.

Bill Gates Channels Bane: I am the League of Shadows

The dismantling the public education system in the USA will the ultimate merger/takeover by the wealthy and powerful with all the standard trademarks of a Wall Street, hostile takeover: layoffs, pension raids, wage and benefits cuts, disdain for the political/legal process, litigation, etc.

Consider how the Common Core Standards, the hair brained scheme of David Coleman, now head of the College Board (SAT testing), and how they came to infiltrate the public and private K-12 education systems of the United States. The national effort to drive those standards into the US education system was bankrolled by The Gates' Foundation with some shifty tactics of the Obama Administration.

According to the Washington Post: "*...the Common Core was instituted in many states without a single vote taken by an elected lawmaker ...The Bill and Melinda Gates Foundation didn't just bankroll the development of what became known as* *the Common Core State Standards. With more than $200 million, the foundation also built political support across the country, persuading state governments to make systemic and costly changes."*

Teachers, parents, students and local school boards were largely bypassed in the Common Core matter. Why common core? Well, in part because businesses want workers with specific noncritical thinking skills. The Common Core, along with P-20 and into workforce performance tracking and database development—also funded by Gates—will allow government and business to track prospects early on and mold them to predetermined employment slots which, in the future, will be scarcer still. America's political, military and economic leaders know well that job openings are dwindling across the USA and much of the world. The demand for jobs is far greater than government and business can supply. It's only going to get worse.

No More Jobs for Human Robots

Indeed, government and business recognizes that expectations for gainful employment and health benefits by the general population, particularly young students and idealistic parents, must be dampened as swiftly as possible to prepare for the dystopian, deterministic republic.

Teaching conformity and non-critical thinking—and surveilling, tracking and recording student performance and acceptance of one's administered role—will be vital to maintaining a society of scarcity. Already, college degrees are declining in value even as they become more expensive for most Americans to get.

US MILITARY'S PROGRESSIVENESS

According to Reich: *"...the demand for well educated workers in the USA seems to have peaked around 2000 and then fallen even as the supply of well educated workers has continued to grow...since 2000 the vast majority of college graduates have experienced little or no gain at all...The achievement gap between poor kids and wealthy kids isn't mainly about race. In fact the racial achievement gap has been narrowing. It is a reflection of the nation's widening gap between poor and wealthy families, of how schools in poor and rich communities are financed, and the nations increasing residential segregation by income...This matters because a large portion of the money to support public schools comes from local property taxes. The federal government provides only about 10 percent of all funding whereas the states contribute 45 percent."*

Ted Trainer offers a reminder of what the real purpose of education is: *"Clearly schools are not there to educate, or we'd check whether that is what they do. They are there to reproduce consumer-capitalist society. That's what everyone wants them to do, and they do it well. That is why schools cannot be fixed. They cannot be reformed to not be riddled with authoritarian relations, pettifogging rules, learning masses of irrelevant and boring stuff, timetables, exams, credentials, failure and human rights abuse. If these features were eliminated then schools would not reproduce consumer-capitalist society."*

The Buzz around Intrexon Corporation: Zika, GMO's, the Pentagon and Wall Street

February 5, 2016: *"Synthetic biology also appears likely to open up opportunities in the human performance modification field through the potential to make regulatory molecules in laboratories or, more directly, inside the body. For example, bacteria that live in the human digestive system already convert food into neurotransmitters and other molecules that influence performance; by engineering these organisms to sense the levels of compounds in the body and to supplement or counteract them when needed, it may be possible to enhance physical, cognitive, and socioemotional (or interpersonal) performance."* **DOD Office of Technical Intelligence**

The mainstream media, the public and financiers are agog over the Zika virus (Zika) which is wreaking havoc on thousands of families and newborns in the vicinity of Piracicaba, Northeast Brazil. Zika cases have already been reported in Texas, Florida and Virginia.

According to the US Center for Disease Control, *"In May 2015, the public health authorities of Brazil confirmed the transmission of Zika virus in the northeast of the country. Since October 2015, other countries and territories of the Americas have reported the presence of the virus."*

Opportunistic Zika is being presented by the mainstream media and some government agencies in the same manner as the beheading of an ISIL/Daesh prisoner, and with all the drama, color commentary and propaganda of the War on Terror, the War in Afghanistan, the War in Iraq, the War on Drugs, the War on Crime, the Cyber War, and the reemerging War against the twin Red—though capitalist—Menaces Russia and China.

US MILITARY'S PROGRESSIVENESS

Is it possible for the United States of America to do anything other than wage war?

At any rate, Piracicaba, Brazil, according to an Intrexon briefing at a JP Morgan sponsored conference, was the site of the "world's first municipality to release Oxitec organisms [genetically modified organisms (GMO's)] into the wild. The organisms were genetically tricked-out male mosquitoes and the release of the flying critters took place in April of 2015. Oxitec is a subsidiary of Intrexon.

The is no established link between Intrexon's release of genetically modified mosquitoes and Zika or the birth defects attributed to Zika that are ravaging the families and children of northeast Brazil. But there is a link, however, between Intrexon's timely purchase of Oxitec in August 2015 for $160 million, and the windfall that Intrexon expects to gain from its genetically modified killer mosquitoes. Already, Wall Street investors, business publications and media outlets are praising the use of GMO's like those of Intrexon's to wipe out malaria, dengue and other diseases even though there remains much scientific uncertainty over the long term effects of inserting GMO's into the ecosystems into which human animals are embedded.

GMO's Taste Great!

Science writer Phillip Ball writes: *"If the idea of introducing a turbo-boosted method of genetic modification into the wild sounds alarming, it should. In 2014, before it was even clear whether gene drives would work in insects, a group of US researchers recommended some safety guidelines and called for regulation and extreme caution before unleashing such a powerful technique in a natural ecosystem. The subsequent publication of a gene-drive system in flies led the same researchers (including those who did that work) to recommend lab containment procedures."*

In similar fashion, another of Intrexon's business units, AquaBounty's AquaAdvantage Salmon, received approval in 2015 from the US Food and Drug Administration to produce and harvest genetically engineered salmon and sell it in the US without warning labels. The GM salmon will be produced in Panama and Canada. However, the US Congress stepped in and indicated that it would not allow the sale of GM salmon in the US without a labeling regime. According to the National Law Review, *"Reversing course from the end of 2015, FDA recently announced an import ban on genetically engineered (GE) salmon until such a time as comprehensive labeling guidelines are introduced. Despite FDA's approval of GE salmon in November 2015, the agency appears to have bowed to congressional pressure and placed a hold on the importation of the AquAdvantage Salmon pending resolution of the labeling guideline controversy."*

Further, documents received by foodandwaterwatch.org through a Freedom of Information Act request reveal that some staff at the US Fish and Wildlife Service expressed reservations about Intrexon's GE salmon and the impact on native salmon: *"...I think the idea of genetically engineered animals that will be consumed is a bad idea anyway but it is done all the time. I think the uncertainty of what will eventually happen to a species if genetically altered animals mix with native stocks is reason enough to oppose this at least until such times as that controlled experimentation takes place...no matter what precautions you take fish escape and once they do, there is no closing that door. So that being said, I think it is a bad precedent to set."*

US MILITARY'S PROGRESSIVENESS
Lobbyists, Genes, Investments and Defense

Sitting on Intrexon's board of directors is Cesar Alvarez of Greenberg Traurig (GT). *"Mr. Alvarez has served since February 2010 as the Executive Chairman of the international law firm of Greenberg Traurig, LLP, and previously served as its Chief Executive Officer from 1997 until his election as Executive Chairman."* If the name Greenberg Traurig sounds familiar, that because it was home to Jack Abramoff who brought in millions of dollars to GT while Alvarez was, ostensibly, in charge as GT's CEO. According to GT's website, *"During his tenure as CEO, which began in 1997, he directed the firm's growth from 325 lawyers in eight offices to approximately 1850 attorneys and government professionals..."* GT has been involved in a number of unsavory activities over the years, many of them under Alvarez's watch.

The Pentagon and US Intelligence agencies are looking into synthetic biology in some sense the way they used to look into hallucinogenic LSD and atomic weapons: Theorize, test on humans, and then see what happens all before regulators get nosy. In January 2015 the Department of Defense's Office of Technical Intelligence produced a report titled Synthetic Biology. The field is described as this: *"Synthetic biology is an emerging field in which scientists modify or 'engineer' DNA to improve their ability to understand, predict, design, and build biological systems...Thus, it is not a new field, but it is new in its approach – holistic engineering of biology – and its promise...Due to DoD's unique missions, there are many special needs for advanced materials, and this area has low regulatory hurdles."*

US MILITARY'S PROGRESSIVENESS

Intrexon gets a few mentions in the Synthetic Biology study, always a good thing for a company looking to relieve the Pentagon's research and engineering units of some cash. Here's one: "*Intrexon, a synthetic biology company that designs and produces organisms for agricultural, medical, and industrial applications, conducted an initial public offering (IPO) this year that valued the company at more than $2 billion.*" Here's another: "*The R&D Services group is similarly young and has received lower levels of investment, with the exception of one big winner: Intrexon, which has attracted $500 million dollars in investment, was omitted from the analysis above because of the degree to which it skews this group.*"

According to opensecrets.org, Supreme Court Justice Samuel Alito has $100,000 to $250,000 "assets" with Intrexon and US Senator Mark Warner has $500,000 to $1,000,000.

Intrexon looks like a buy!

US MILITARY'S PROGRESSIVENESS
Colonialism via Data, Sensors, Genes, Neuroscience

March 12, 2016: In 2007 I wrote and presented a conceptual paper to an international studies group in Portugal. The subject matter was, generally, the use of Evolutionary Cognitive Neuroscience (ECN) to manage humanity. That paper would eventually finds its way, remarkably, into Rebecca Costa's seminal The Watchman's Rattle.

I said back in 2007 that America's ongoing obsession with national security and the enormous funding necessary to soothe a national psyche of fear and war was a key driver for enhancing security thereby eliminating the uncertainty of daily living. I suggested that ECN could generate predictive and diagnostic biotechnologies to reduce tension. Such a development could eliminate much uncertainty and concomitant drama in human affairs by providing leaders with assets to manage the complexities in brain-behavior relationships. To get there though, reliable data on human beings, as they function as interconnected consumers, warfighters, enemies, refugees, diplomats, criminals, and citizens of their respective nations would need to be collected and assessed.

I went on to say that a comprehensive knowledge base of planetary ecosystems and how humans interface with those ecosystems would have to be constructed and meshed with the findings of brain-behavior functions. The dissection of the individual and global organism may lead to unprecedented forecasting capability with the ultimate outcome the creation of biomachine systems that suggest procedures and diagnostics with which to anticipate and/or minimize a wide range of human problems. Biomachine tools might become available that could suggest courses of action such as military intervention, diplomacy, containment, stability and consequence management operations, economic aid, covert operations, etc. I also briefly mentioned that one of the dangers in such a pursuit would likely be the development of neuroweaponry.

In just under ten years, the topics alluded to in my 2007 paper have taken the form of four converging and accelerating movements that seem likely to usher in drastic change in the human condition: The digitization of human behavior; cracking open the brain through neuroscience; the engineering and manipulation of human and non-human genomes; and the proliferation of the Internet of Things, which is code for the sensorization of the human/non-human, home, work, school, automobile, street and global commons.

Is it any surprise that the Anthropocene is upon us?

What Happens Next?

Shoshana Zuboff, in the article, The Secrets of Surveillance Capitalism, thinks that humanity will become mentally displaced, perhaps disembodied, as behavior becomes totally predictable and free will vanishes.

"The significance of behavioral surplus was quickly camouflaged, both at Google and eventually throughout the Internet industry, with labels like "digital exhaust," "digital breadcrumbs,"... These euphemisms for behavioral surplus operate as ideological filters, in exactly the same way that the earliest maps of the North American continent labeled whole regions with terms like "heathens," "infidels," "idolaters," "primitives," "vassals," or "rebels." On the strength of those labels, native peoples, their places and claims, were erased from the invaders' moral and legal equations, legitimating

their acts of taking and breaking in the name of Church and Monarchy. We are the native peoples now whose tacit claims to self-determination have vanished from the maps of our own behavior. They are erased in an astonishing and audacious act of dispossession by surveillance that claims its right to ignore every boundary in its thirst for knowledge of and influence over the most detailed nuances of our behavior. For those who pondered about the logical completion of the global processes of commodification, the answer is that they complete themselves in the dispossession of our intimate quotidian reality, now reborn as behavior to be monitored and modified, bought and sold."

Radar Love

Social Radar has been a goal of the government and business for some time. Its applications are legion: Predictive behavioral algorithms to ensure consumers are directed to the right product to ensure steady profits; underlying predictive mathematical models that allow the military commander a quantitative, geospatial view of open or urban terrain with humans moving predictably like aircraft on an air traffic controller's screen; and the creation of a predictive reality in which the masses believe they are "free", but are, unknown to them, being behaviorally shaped for the larger system.

These notions can be found in military doctrine and a host of academic and marketing organizations. It's all there out in the open if anyone cares to look.

Let's consider The MITRE Corporation's development of Social Radar. In Social Radar for Smart Power, Mark Maybury writes: *"Conventional radar requires signatures for different kinds of objects and events: it needs to be tuned to different environmental conditions to provide accurate and reliable information. Analogously a social radar needs signatures, calibration, and correlation to sense, if not forecast, a broad spectrum of phenomena (e.g., political, economic, social, environmental, health) and potentially forecast changing trends in population perceptions and behaviors. For example, radar or sonar enable some degree of forecasting by tracking spatial and temporal patterns (e.g. they track and display how military objects or weather phenomena move in what clusters, in which direction(s) and at what speed.) A user can thus project where and when objects will be in the future. Similarly, a social radar should enable us to forecast who will cluster with whom in a network, where, and when in what kinds of relationships...Public Opinion Polling by Proxy (POP/P) [is] an exploration of the ability of social media (e.g., Twitter) to serve as a proxy for traditional opinion polling methods to overcome their latency, expense, and invasiveness."*

If We Kick the Ant Hill, Where will the Ants Go?

The US national security community's dream is to have a Social Radar like the one described above by Maybury that would allow military commanders to lord over other countries. The Pentagon's Sociocultural Behavior Research and Engineering in a Department of Defense Context contains this statement: *"Mastery would mean that US forces would have the data on indigenous populations and the training they need to move easily in those populations; could see the parameters of culture and society and integrate those with conventional mapping of the physical terrain; could detect often complex and dynamic networks, where adversaries and civilian populations are intermingled; and would possess non-kinetic tools as well as the ability to anticipate both the near-term and long-term impacts of applying those tools."*

US MILITARY'S PROGRESSIVENESS

It's easy to pick on the Pentagon on these matters, of course. But the insidious reality is that for profit, commercial enterprises with global reach—and the many lobbyists and non-profits who work on their behalf to distort regulatory regimes designed to oversee their activities—must modify human behavior in order to control/corner global markets, turn a profit and survive. These are the new colonialists who now brandish the US military as a tool for their own ends.

If Zuboff is correct, then Google–and corporations colluding with them—are engaging in a type of intellectual property theft from unwitting customers. The thoughts, feelings, and the sense of individual uniqueness of a human being (or his/her genetic structure) ultimately will end up getting copyrighted, trademarked or patented by corporations. It is the Internet of Sensors, Neuroscience, Genetic Engineering and the Digitization of Earth in the techno-dictatorial hands of corporate boardrooms and financiers that may well prove to be apocalyptic for all life on Earth.

The leadership of the dangerously privatized US military has become an extension of this techno-corporate collective and the governing civilians the collective owns. Indeed, so much so that US military leadership, while on "active duty", emulates its mentors in the corporate world because (a.) rampant internal privatization has distorted the US military; and (b.) the private sector is where US military leaders long to be when it's retirement time. It's all about networking for the big payday in the private sector, or developing networking diagrams to see who the bad guys affiliate with in some remote corner of the African continent.

So it is no surprise that: *"...the worldview that governs the U.S military's approach...is one where populations are de-coded as networks. To see like the twenty-first century US military is to see a world of networks. This world of networks is a secular cosmological vision derivative from the human-machine assemblages where US military personnel and institutions are imbricated. These human-machine assemblages have been violently extended...through new technologies like iris-scan biometrics devices and data-base management...many new twenty-first century technologies, like big data mining and computational social network analysis, are rooted in colonial practices."* **The Afterlives of Counterinsurgency: Post Colonialism, Military Social Science, and Afghanistan 2006-2012 by Oliver Christian Belcher**

Hillary Clinton Channels Allen and John Foster Dulles: Is the Clinton Foundation the Dulles Brother's Sullivan and Cromwell?

April 15, 2016: *"The desire for secrecy is one of Mrs. Clinton's enduring and damaging traits…Befitting a Midwestern Methodist with a bullying father, repression has always been one of Mrs. Clinton's most prominent characteristics. Hers has been the instinct to conceal, to deny, to refuse to admit any mistake. Mickey Kantor, the Los Angeles lawyer who worked on the 1992 [presidential] campaign, said that Hillary adamantly refused to admit to any mistakes. Since Vietnam, there's never been a war that Mrs. Clinton didn't like. She argued passionately in the White House for the NATO bombing of Belgrade. Five days after September 11, 2001, she was calling for a broad war on terror… "I'll stand behind [George W.] Bush for a long time to come", Senator Clinton promised, and she was as good as her word, voting for the Patriot Act and the wide-ranging authorization to use military force against Afghanistan…Of course she supported without reservation the attack on Afghanistan and, as the propaganda buildup toward the onslaught on Iraq got underway, she didn't even bother to walk down the hall to read the national intelligence estimate on Iraq before the war."* **Counterpunch editors Alexander Cockburn and Jeffrey St. Clair**

As Secretary of State, Hillary Clinton instigated and legitimized the overthrow of the Honduran government in 2009 similar to the 1954 Guatemala Coup engineered primarily by CIA Director Allen Dulles, supported by Secretary of State John Foster Dulles, and with the glowing approval of President Dwight Eisenhower.

US MILITARY'S PROGRESSIVENESS

In a March 2016 interview with Amy Goodman on Democracy Now, Greg Grandin, a professor of Latin American history at New York University, discussed the fallout from the 2009 Honduran Coup. *"I mean hundreds of peasant activists and indigenous activists have been killed. Scores of gay rights activists have been killed. I mean, it's just—it's just a nightmare in Honduras. I mean, there's ways in which the coup regime basically threw up Honduras to transnational pillage. And Berta Cáceres [a prominent Honduran activist assassinated in 2016], in that interview, says what was installed after the coup was something like a permanent counterinsurgency on behalf of transnational capital. And that was—that wouldn't have been possible if it were not for Hillary Clinton's normalization of that election, or legitimacy."*

In an April interview with Dana Frank, professor of history at the University of California, Santa Cruz, on Democracy Now, Frank indicated that President Obama had basically turned over Central and South America to Hillary Clinton.

Frank then said this: *"I think it's really about the US pushback against the democratically elected governments of the left and the center-left that came to power in Latin America in the '90s and in the 2000s—Venezuela, Bolivia, Argentina, Ecuador, Chile, El Salvador, all these countries. And Zelaya was the weakest link in that chain. He, himself, did not come out of a big social movement base at the time of his election, certainly since the coup. And I think they were—the US was looking for a way to push back against that. There's a very important military base, U.S military base, Soto Cano Air Force Base, in Honduras. And Honduras has always been the most captive nation of the United States in Latin America. So, I think they were testing what they could get away with. And they got away with it. It was the first domino pushing back against democracy in Latin America and reasserting U.S. power, in service to a transnational corporate agenda."*

It's Not Your Country or Life

The 1954 coup that ousted Guatemalan President Jacob Arbenz from the presidency had the same rationale as Hillary Clinton's 21st Century Honduran effort. David Talbot, writing in the must-read book The Devil's Chessboard: Allen Dulles, the CIA and the Rise of America's Secret Government, noted that Arbenz's mistake was antagonizing the United Fruit Company by attempting to *"expropriate acreage from the United Fruit Company's large holding that were not under cultivation, and [Arbenz] had offered the multinational corporation fair compensation for the seized land."*

But United Fruit had powerful connections in the Eisenhower Administration. John Foster Dulles had long been a legal advisor to United Fruit for many years. Both brothers held shares of stock in the company. Robert Cutler, head of Eisenhower's National Security Council, was the former chair of United Fruit. Walter "Beetle" Smith, former CIA director and close friend of Eisenhower, would end up on the United Fruit Board of Directors after the coup. Even Eisenhower's personal secretary, Ann Whitman, was affiliated with United Fruit: her husband was its publicity director. Other violent overthrows of foreign governments and the destruction of their societies for crass business and career interests would be coated by Allen Dulles in layers of red paint; that is, Communist red paint. Murder, extortion, coups, wars, torture, oppression, censorship, lies, theft, profits, racism, threat exaggeration and evil leadership would be legitimized under the guise of national security during the Cold War.

US MILITARY'S PROGRESSIVENESS

According to Talbot, *"By the time the bloodletting had run its course [in Guatemala], four decades later, over 250,000 people had been killed in a nation whose total population was less than four million when the reign of terror began."*

For many years the Dulles brothers were ensured the support of the gatekeepers in banking, finance, media, the military and the US Congress through relationships made and sealed during World War I, the interwar years, and World War II. The Nazi's would serve the Dulles brothers well in their private and public roles. Allen would direct the merger of the CIA with some of the worst elements of the defeated Third Reich. John Foster who while at Sullivan and Cromwell pushed back against closing its satellite office in Nazi Germany often advocated that nuclear weapons should be viewed as conventional weapons. In some sense, the two brothers seemed to possess the same zealousness and cruelty of the Third Reich.

Near WWII's end, Allen protected Nazi intelligence chief for the Eastern Front, Major General Reinhard Gehlen, from war crimes trials and would later merge Gehlen's operatives and network into the CIA's operation. Gehlen would become the first chief of West German intelligence (BND) and hold the position until 1968. Allen also cut clandestine deals with other Nazi's—government officials, bankers, scientists, researchers, et al–through various operations like PAPERCLIP and SUNRISE. Nazi expertise was used in experimental brain/cognitive modification via ARTICHOKE and MKULTRA. Talbot speculates, chillingly, that Allen was connected with the assassination of John F. Kennedy and not only via his critical role on the Warren Commission. Talbot documents the frenetic activity at the ex-CIA director's residence in Georgetown, Washington, DC, prior to 22 November 1963. He also notes Allen's encampment at "The

Farm"—a clandestine training center on the CIA campus—
from 22 to 24 November 1963.

It's a Good Day for Someone Else to Die Hard

According to Consortium News, when Hillary Clinton was
asked about the death of Muammar Qaddafi, Libya's deposed
ruler, at the hands of a mob, she said, "We came, we saw, he
died." That's a comment Allen Dulles–or a psychopath–might
have made. That's worrisome in a world in which President
Hillary Clinton may become a reality.

Her penchant for war, secrecy and cover-up, Yale pedigree and
alumni network, corporate connections from Wall Street to
London, fealty to Israel, shapeshifting Republican/Democrat
persona, and the use of the Clinton Foundation as a sort of non-
profit, quasi-government, global intelligence/networking
agency makes comparing her with the Dulles brothers—and
their public/private lives, not as crazy as it first seems. The
Clinton Foundation has initiatives in dozens of countries
throughout the world. Its connections in international corporate
board rooms and the principals of foreign national and local
governance give it access to information/intelligence. It is also
involved in US political campaigns indirectly through its
donors.

For example, one of the Clinton Foundation's board members
is Frank Guistra. According to a 2013 Huffington Post article,
*"Clinton was borrowing [Giustra's private jet] to begin a four-
day speaking tour of Latin America that would pay him
$800,000…Frank Giustra was forming a friendship that would
make him part of the former president's inner circle and gain
him introductions to presidents of Kazakhstan and Colombia…
Giustra's self-serving philanthropy also took him and Clinton*

to Kazakhstan in September 2007, as documented in a January 2008 New York Times investigation... Within two days [of the beginning of the trip], corporate records show that Mr. Giustra also came up a winner when his company [UrAsia Energy Ltd.] signed preliminary agreements giving it the right to buy into three uranium projects controlled by Kazakhstan's state-owned uranium agency, Kazatomprom,"...The monster deal stunned the mining industry, turning an unknown shell company [UrAsia] into one of the world's largest uranium producers in a transaction ultimately worth tens of millions of dollars to Mr. Giustra....Just months after the Kazakh pact was finalized, Mr. Clinton's charitable foundation received its own windfall: a $31.3 million donation from Mr. Giustra... Within a year and a half, Giustra sold off his stake in the Kazatomprom joint venture for $3.1 billion, which he had originally purchased for $450 million."

In a 2015 Washington Post piece, the governor of the Virginia, Terry McAuliffe, *"More than 175 contributors to the Clinton Foundation and to Hillary Rodham Clinton's 2016 Democratic presidential campaign have dug deep into their wallets for McAuliffe (Democrat), often giving prolifically despite little or no connection to Virginia...Among them is an Omaha database executive who lavished so much corporate jet travel on himself and the Clinton family that shareholders forced him out, Hollywood media mogul with a singular interest in Israel, and an Argentine-born energy tycoon who recalled visiting Richmond just once — flying in and out years ago with Bill Clinton, his Georgetown classmate. Of the $60 million McAuliffe has raised for his two gubernatorial bids, inauguration, political action committee and the Democratic Party of Virginia, nearly $18 million has come from* *contributors to the Clinton Foundation or to Hillary Clinton's current campaign.* "

US MILITARY'S PROGRESSIVENESS
US Military More Secure, Progressive

July 20, 2016: Law enforcement officers were ambushed and killed in Baton Rouge and Dallas by those using unconventional warfare tactics. Is this any different that the Sunni "terrorists" who killed US soldiers in Iraq?

How about the Nice, France truck bomber? Was he any different from Timothy McVeigh who parked a truck bomb outside the Murrah Federal Building in Oklahoma City killing 168 and wounding scores more?

Nearly 16,000 Americans murdered each year by each other. Are not murderer's terrorists?

The United States is a country that seems to be at war with itself, politically polarized and rigidly classed to the point that lyrics in the 1960s songs like Steppenwolf's Monster and the Temptations' Ball of Confusion speak directly to the developing catastrophe to come.

What's the Matter?

First Peoples, Latino, Black, Jewish, Asian, White, Transgender, Gay, Lesbian, Bisexual, Catholic, Wiccan, Protestant, Muslim, Heterosexual, Arab, Amish, Persian, lives matter and so do many non-human lives. But there are so many lives-that-matter interest groups, whose members work in every profession in America—legal and not—with so many divergent and cultural agendas, that it is impossible for anyone in any leadership position from gang leader to political leader to placate them all.

And with each passing day they fear the other groups that matter. Blacks fear cops, cops fear for their lives from all the matter groups. Muslims deride the Christian and Jewish of the Book as infidels.

Some matter groups want punitive damages paid to them for sins committed by slavery and racial exclusion for nearly 200 years. Others seek to exterminate Western European and US infidels by beheadings and acts of terror and restore the world as it was 500 years ago. Some orthodox matter groups normally called cults, seek isolation from the general population, discourage interaction with it, and yet reap the rewards that a relatively stable, secure country provides.

Still others, those gilded stovepipe denizens, who claim to inhale air more purified—therefore leading to clearer thinking—believe the remainder say 90 percent of the populace, to be knuckle dragging humans who need to be collared and led to a promised land. They have a Moses complex that leads them to believe they are the only ones sanctioned to speak with God, or lead the tribe.

And there are the religions that matter who seek to maintain their churches and cathedrals by coercing the followers to go to those buildings to worship as necessary when scripture maintains it is not.

I apologize here concerning Moses because I don't know what type of matter Moses was besides that he led the Jewish people out of Egypt. Perhaps he was one of the letters of this acronym: LGBT. Maybe he was a feminist supporter. Maybe he was black.

And I also apologize to Allah and Krishna and to the Christian God and Satan because I don't really know who is in charge.

I must do penance too because I am white and I'm writing on the white background on MS Word and all the letters and numbers are white too. The clouds floating in the sky are white and the pages of the books the Bible, Koran, Bhagavad Gita and Maurice Blanchot's, The Infinite Conversation that sit atop my nightstand, are all white too. Of course I am male too and that means I carry inherent bias against women too and anyone else but my demographic.

Scattered Matter

With American society on the verge of exploding like the Big Bang, there does not seem to be a centralizing force to keep it together. So what now?

Can't we get along? No way. Our hands must be forced and we must be disciplined if the madness is to stop.

What happens when the standing Army, military forces, become more progressive than civilian society? When the US military leaves the civilian sector behind in terms of diversity, identity, then what? It is a world unto itself, a sort of strange idealized world the civilian realm can't be. All the matter groups are represented in the US national security machinery— even the closet terrorist–yet they are forced; indeed, agree when they become military personnel, to obey orders, get along, or get out. It's a radical change for the institution and serves as a model on forcing people together with authority.

There is even a Wicca worship site at the USAF academy. In one form or another, all the matter groups are celebrated openly at the Pentagon in Washington, D C, most recently the T in LGBT. Muslims are honored. First Peoples, women, Latino and blacks are praised openly.

US MILITARY'S PROGRESSIVENESS

Humans are, in the end, a nasty species. We kill each other because we think we matter more than the Other. We deceive at every turn in the interests of ourselves, family, friends or belief. We even destroy fellow non-human creatures with impunity. We are undisciplined, disinclined to political discourse and favor the mind-numbing delights of television. Here in America we are armchair citizens active on the World Wide Web, not in communities or the streets.

And we actually do not find it a "guilty pleasure" any longer to watch the killings, beheadings, and suffering on the television. It's a pleasure, now with the thinking something like this: I can't wait to kick back in my chair with IPhone, laptop and TV on so I can watch cop shooting whites, blacks, Latino's, Asians, Arabs; the latest terrorist acts around the globe; video footage of drone strikes; "expert" blatherskites hawking their banalities on the news networks; and then, of course, the latest episode of Naked and Afraid.

US Presidential Race 2016: Cruella de Vil versus Captain Klutz

August 10, 2016: The world knows that the 2016 US presidential horse race features two cartoonish characters that are perhaps the most polarizing, distasteful figures in recent American national politics. Hillary Clinton and Donald Trump appear at a tenuous moment in the world's history as economies struggle, infrastructure collapses, nations crumble, and the political systems, at least in the US and Europe, are viewed with disdain by a majority of citizens.

In the USA, the drumbeats for war seem to be getting louder. US Secretary of Defense Ash Carter uses a truncated version of David Letterman's Top Ten List to rank the most dangerous threats to the USA: 1. Russia; 2. China; 3 Iran; 4. North Korea; and 5. Islamic State/Terrorism. The demonization of Russia and the references to Islamic State as a cancer or virus recalls Whitehead's Cannibal War Machine. Yet, threats to the nation remain and must be dealt with.

Like or hate Trump, the media bias against him for challenging the neoliberal order is astonishing, harkening back to Cold War media propaganda He is vilified out of fear he might shake the old order up: Reorder NATO, work with the Russian president, focus money on US infrastructure.

US Crushing it in Asymmetric Information War

The US is waging a highly successful asymmetric war against Russia which that country can hardly match given the US Instruments of National Power (INP), one of which includes "media" under the INP "Information." The mainstream media propaganda campaign against Russia has been so successful

136

that a Russian swimmer who served a suspension for illegal drug use and was cleared to compete in Rio was booed by fans and publicly admonished by an American swimmer. The US does not even want the viewing public to see the flag of Russia raised during an NBC broadcast at the US Olympic Games. US sportscasters, and their counterparts in US owned media outlets in South America, pound into the viewing public's collective minds that Russia is "enemy number one." The penetration of the DNC computer network blamed on Russia comes at a moment when US dominated media coverage of the Olympics can be used to amplify the information warfare campaign against Russia and its comrades in Carter's Top Five enemies list.

The New York Times, Washington Post, mainstream/cable news reek of polemic and government "officials" in a stunning disinformation campaign while at the same time they try to dismiss Clinton's continued flirtation with the FBI/IRS over email, the shenanigans of the Clinton Foundation, and her militaristic "love a man in uniform", and her coup instigating past. Even former military commanders and the CIA have gotten in on 2016 presidential campaign.

General Martin Dempsey, USA (Ret.)–former chair of the Joint Chiefs of Staff (JCS)—and General Joseph Dunford, USMC, and current chair of JCS, are so alarmed at this development that they publicly warned military personnel about getting involved, vocally, in the 2016 presidential election.

US MILITARY'S PROGRESSIVENESS
Sharknado

This all has the feel of a Sharknado movie or better still, a nutty cartoon. Perhaps it is better to think of Clinton and Trump as the cartoon characters they are.

Cruella de Vil was the evil female villain in 101 Dalmatians. She is described by Wikipedia as being "the tyrannical figure in the marriage, and her husband as a meek, subservient man who seldom speaks and obeys his wife entirely. Cruella expresses her sinister interest in the Dalmatians, remarking how she and her henpecked husband have never thought of making clothing from dog pelt before. Yet seeing the spotless skins of the newborn puppies she is revolted and offers to have them drowned at once; her way of getting rid of animals she views as worthless, including dozens of her own cat's kittens. Upon a second visit to the house she picks up the mature puppies and treats them like clothing to be worn."

Replace puppies with 70 percent of the US population and you get a fine sense of what she really thinks about the vast majority of Americans. If she had her way she'd get the names of all the citizens who will vote for Trump and have them pilloried or sent to the gulag.

Trump is the Captain Klutz of the US political scene. He is running close to Cruella in spite of his wacky statements and the clumsy carnival that is his campaign. It is like watching a bizarre Saturday Night Live episode (one in which Trump appeared).

Captain Klutz, or Ringo Fonebone, can't handle the "normal" life, according to a Lutz fan site: Klutz "usually succeeded in capturing the bad guy in spite of himself. As a child, Fonebone did nothing other than read Brap Man, The Blue Blockhead,

Baboon Boy, and other comic books, leaving him with little aptitude for normal human activities."

Trump is a bona fide member of the US 1 Percent having lived anything but a normal human life and who knows what his reading list included. His gaffs somehow earn him more supporters, like Captain Klutz's goofball actions help save the day.

Klutz remains within 15 percentage points of Cruella in spite of the unprecedented opposition to a presidential candidate in recent US history.

Hillary "Cruella" Clinton will be the next president of the United States. She will helm a socially fractured, polarized, identity-biased "Matters" country. To reconstitute the USA, she will create a war that every American can agree on.

Trump, or at least his supporters, and frustrated Sanders followers will play a pivotal role in the mayhem that is to come.

Brzezinski Vision for a Power Sharing World Stymied by Ignorant Americans Leaders, Citizens

August 27, 2016: *"A constructive U.S. policy must be patiently guided by a long-range vision. The alternative…and especially the quest for a one-sided militarily and ideologically imposed outcome, can only result in prolonged and self-destructive futility. For America, that could entail enduring conflict, fatigue, and conceivably even a demoralizing withdrawal to its pre-20th century isolationism. For Russia, it could mean major defeat, increasing the likelihood of subordination in some fashion to Chinese predominance. For China, it could portend war not only with the United States but also, perhaps separately, with either Japan or India or with both. And, in any case, a prolonged phase of sustained ethnic, quasi-religious wars pursued through the Middle East with self-righteous fanaticism would generate escalating bloodshed within and outside the region, and growing cruelty everywhere."*
Towards a Global Realignment, The National Interest, Z. Brzezinski, 2016

*"[American exceptionalism] is a reaction to the inability of people to understand global complexity or important issues like American energy dependency. They search for simplistic sources of comfort and clarity. And the people that they are now selecting to be, so to speak, the spokespersons of their anxieties are, in most cases, stunningly ignorant."***Interview Spiegel ONLINE, 2010**

"Since the next twenty years may well be the last phase of the more traditional and familiar political alignments with which we have grown comfortable, the response needs to be shaped now. During the rest of this century, humanity will also have to be increasingly preoccupied with survival as such on account

of a confluence of environmental challenges. Those challenges can only be addressed responsibly and effectively in a setting of increased international accommodation. And that accommodation has to be based on a strategic vision that recognizes the urgent need for a new geopolitical framework. " **Brzezinski, 2016**

"I am very worried that most Americans are close to total ignorance about the world. They are ignorant. That is an unhealthy condition... " **Interview Spiegel ONLINE, Brzezinski, 2010**

Zbigniew Brzezinski's likely to be prophetic piece Towards a Global Alignment sets forth what he believes to be the likely future geopolitical construct which will see the USA-Europe, China and Russia as the dominant global powers and regional powers on the world stage. There is no guarantee of this outcome if the USA does not lead the way in constructing such a world through an altruistic approach to sharing power with its many former adversaries. A US national security strategy that seeks lopsided military and economic global power over its challengers is doomed to fail in the long term, the former national security advisor thinks.

Whoops! Forgot About India

Brzezinski has neglected to include India in his Nostradamian thesis. Narendra Modi, India's prime minister, has taken a page out of China's playbook and is cutting trade deals with regional neighbors as well as Russia and the USA. India seeks to boost exports as it desperately needs to export more to boost income at home.

India is hedging its bets with China, keeping a wary eye on the China-Pakistan relationship, and like other G-20 member states, doing some chest thumping before that group meets on September 4. India's Act East Policy seeks to tighten economic and diplomatic ties with the ASEAN countries. Modi's defense minister Manohar Parrikar is set to visit Washington, DC, shortly to sign agreements allowing the US to use Indian military bases for logistics and humanitarian operations, maritime cooperation and cybersecurity. He also is bringing a wish list of military equipment India seeks to purchase from defense giants Lockheed and Boeing. India is also in the market for the latest technologies included on the new US Ford Class aircraft carriers (advanced radars and electromagnetic aircraft launch systems) for its own indigenous brand of carrier. And it has cozied up to the US position on the South China Sea which most assuredly has upset Chinese leadership.

So India is clearly making an attempt become the fourth power pole with USA-Europe, Russia and China.

In Other News

Meanwhile, in the background, China has broken with its history and will now join the melee in Syria in a humanitarian or military advisory capacity. The July 15 attempt to overthrow the Turkish government is still reverberating across Western Asia. Afghanistan, Yemen, Iraq, Libya and Syria are little more than piles of rubble as 2016 comes to a close. The Islamic State is set to be pulverized anywhere is exists and any civilians or intact structures in close proximity to Daesh will be eliminated. The internally displaced and refugee populations continues to grow in ebbs and flows and is taxing the governments and citizens of Europe, Lebanon, Iran and Turkey. Add to this boiling stew the USA's own immigration issues with Mexico and Central America, a stumbling global economy and climate change and it's no wonder people everywhere are nervous drawing comparisons to events leading up to both WWI and WWII.

Secretary of Defense Ash Carter typically mentions some of these matters in his speeches and always reminds his audiences that the top five threats, in order of danger, are Russia, China, Iran, North Korea and the Islamic State, and terrorism in general.

Russia is listed as US Public Enemy #1 and, because of its nuclear capabilities, is, indeed a threat. In conventional military terms, it does not pose a global threat, nor can it match the $14-16 trillion in GDP the US pumps out each year.

Both nations are modernizing their nuclear triads. But Russia can't match penny for penny, or technologically, the onslaught of US development and deployment of ground based strategic deterrent (GBSD) ICBM's to replace silo based Minuteman III's, long range strategic nuke cruise missiles, the Northrop Grumman B-21 bombers, upgrades to nuclear weapons equipped subs, or the fielding upgraded B-61 nuclear bombs in Europe in the coming decade. To top it all off, the Lockheed Martin F-35 Strike Fighter is slowly making its way into combat.

Looking beneath the current issues are the flames ignited by the historical activity set by the three power centers Brzezinski believes must settle the world: USA-Europe, China and Russia. As an aside, India's hatred-of-others quotient is noticeable as its defense minister recently said, "Going to Pakistan is the same as going to hell."

At any rate, Brzezinski explains why Americans, Europeans and Russians are loathed by so many in every corners of the globe. It's worth quoting him extensively on this point because it is a remarkable statement/admission coming from someone who designed the Carter Doctrine which is responsible for embroiling the USA in so many conflicts in the Persian Gulf region.

"Periodic massacres of their not-so-distant ancestors by colonists and associated wealth-seekers largely from western Europe resulted within the past two or so centuries in the slaughter of colonized peoples on a scale comparable to Nazi World War II crimes. Let just a few examples suffice. In the 16th century, due largely to disease brought by Spanish explorers, the population of the native Aztec Empire in present-day Mexico declined from 25 million to approximately one million.

Similarly, in North America, an estimated 90 percent of the native population died within the first five years of contact with European settlers, due primarily to diseases. In the 19th century, various wars and forced resettlements killed an additional 100,000. In India from 1857-1867, the British are suspected of killing up to one million civilians in reprisals stemming from the Indian Rebellion of 1857. The British East India Company's use of Indian agriculture to grow opium then essentially forced on China resulted in the premature deaths of millions, not including the directly inflicted Chinese casualties of the First and Second Opium Wars. In the Congo, which was the personal holding of Belgian King Leopold II, 10-15 million people were killed between 1890 and 1910. In Vietnam, recent estimates suggest that between one and three million civilians were killed from 1955 to 1975.

As to the Muslim world in Russia's Caucasus, from 1864 and 1867, 90 percent of the local Circassian population was forcibly relocated and between 300,000 and 1.5 million either starved to death or were killed. Between 1916 and 1918, tens of thousands of Muslims were killed when 300,000 Turkic Muslims were forced by Russian authorities through the mountains of Central Asia and into China. In Indonesia, between 1835 and 1840, the Dutch occupiers killed an estimated 300,000 civilians.

In Algeria, following a 15-year civil war from 1830-1845, French brutality, famine, and disease killed 1.5 million Algerians, nearly half the population. In neighboring Libya, the Italians forced Cyrenaicans into concentration camps, where an estimated 80,000 to 500,000 died between 1927 and 1934. More recently, in Afghanistan between 1979 and 1989 the Soviet Union is estimated to have killed around one million civilians; two decades later, the United States has killed 26,000 civilians during its 15-year war in Afghanistan. In Iraq, 165,000 civilians have been killed by the United States and its allies in the past 13 years."

America: Home of the Stupid but Mean Well People

Brzezinski states that the USA must tame this beastly world and that's only going to work if it shares the leadership mantle it has held for so long. But his own legitimate concerns with the intelligence of America's leaders and its people and their ability to deal with complex matters at home and abroad suggests that the USA will likely reach back to the heady post 911 days during which "full spectrum dominance" of the world was the USA's mission.

Hillary Clinton and Donald Trump are both tragicomic circus acts polluting the airwaves with banalities and clichés lending weight to Brzezinski's thesis that the USA and its leaders are stunningly ignorant. The US media machine, beginning with its sickening support for the 2003 Iraq War and now ending with its equally horrid coverage of the US presidential campaign and its practice of squalid 1950s anti-Russian and Chinese, dumbs down the American populace even further.

It is dark in the USA. There is not a leader or citizen brain in the country with a lightbulb on, or that can be switched on, to deal with the issues of the day.

Perhaps this is why Deep States or Shadow, Double Governments exist.

And maybe this is why soft/hard coups happen.

Cyber Hustlers The Atlantic Council and the New York Times Say Americans Stupid, Military Incompetent

October 4, 2016: *"There is an inverse relationship between public access to the Internet and the inability of governments and institutions to control information flow and hence state allegiance, ideology, public opinion, and policy formulation. Increase in public access to the Internet results in an equivalent decrease in government and institutional power. Indeed, after September 11, 2001, Internet traffic statistics show that many millions of Americans have connected to alternative news sources outside the continental United States. The information they consume can be and often is contrary to US government statements and US mainstream media reporting. Recognizing this, terrorists will coordinate their assaults with an adroit use of cyberspace for the purpose of manipulating perceptions, opinion, and the political and socioeconomic direction of many nation-states."* **John Stanton, Terrorists Will Exploit and Widen the Gap between Governing Structures and the Public, American Behavioral Scientist, 2002**

"Information is a strategic resource vital to national security. US Government efforts to understand and engage key audiences to create, strengthen, or preserve conditions favorable for the advancement of USG interests, policies, and objectives through coordinated programs, plans, themes, messages, and products synchronized with the actions of all elements of national power: Diplomacy, Intelligence, Military, Economic, Finance, Law Enforcement, Information... The DOD must also support and participate in USG Strategic C communications activities to understand, inform, and influence

relevant foreign audiences, including the DOD's transition to and from hostilities, security, military forward presence, and stability operations." **US Army Unconventional Warfare Manual, 2008**

In the early 1990s scores of studies were conducted by the US government, think tanks, consulting firms, defense contractors, futurists and military thinkers on the likely threats to the US military's electronic communications systems. Those analyses often encompassed commercial networked systems.

For example, in May 1993 Security Measures for Wireless Communications was released under the auspices of the US National Communications System. Not long after, the same office published The Electronic Intrusion Threat to National Security and Emergency Preparedness in December 1994. During June 1995 a conference, co-sponsored by the Technical Marketing Society of America, was held. That event was titled Information Warfare: Addressing the Revolutionary New Paradigm for Modern Warfare.

Then as now the most pernicious and non-life threatening cyber-attacks normally resulted in the theft of identities and, perhaps, intellectual property to which 'experts' would assign dollar values. Other network, computer assaults were visited upon databases containing personal information producing headaches for the individuals who had to get new credit cards or revise identities. Embarrassment was the penalty for commercial organizations too cheap to invest in robust electronic security systems.

I Love New York

Information Operations have not taken place (yet) resulting in large scale, life-threatening fallout, but the 1977 New York

City blackout provides some clues as to what might result from a successful cyber assault on a power grid. Those initially responsible for the Black Out were bolts of lightning from a thunderstorm that repeatedly struck a Consolidated Edison facility. Redundancies built into the grid that did not function and aging equipment and operator error led to the loss of power. Observers were already thinking about rudimentary network centric themes even then as The Trigger Effect from the 1978 series Connections by James Burke demonstrates.

It is difficult to say with any certainty if, over the last 23 years, competently secured US military networks have been successfully compromised by electronic intrusions by noted Information Warfare nations Russia, China and Israel seeking to steal classified, compartmented data or Intelligence, Surveillance and Reconnaissance technologies. That information is not likely to ever see the light of day, classified as it should be.

Certainly, US military websites and other government organizations have been hacked successfully over the years resulting in detrimental data spills and website defacement. But these do not rise to the level of national security threat; instead, they are clear cut cases of robbery and vandalism and should be viewed from a civilian law enforcement perspective.

Insiders Have Done More Damage to US National Security

It is worth noting that, to date, the most serious breaches of US national and military security have come at the hands of disillusioned US citizens like Jonathan Pollard (US Navy) and Richard Hansen (FBI) who lifted paper documents from secure facilities, and Edward Snowden (NSA & Booz Allen) who downloaded electronic files to his storage devices.

US MILITARY'S PROGRESSIVENESS

As far as anyone knows, the electromagnetic waves emanating from a computer display have not been remotely manipulated by a state or non-state actor to kill or maim a person looking at the display. But transmitting retroviral software at some distance, or using an intelligence operative to insert destructive code via a flash drive, is known to have been successful in the US-led operation against Iran as the Stuxent case demonstrated.

Recent electronic intrusions and theft of data/images from the non-secured private accounts of former NATO commander General Phillip Breedlove, USAF (Ret.); Andrew Weiner (sexting former politician from New York) or General Colin Powell, USA (Ret.) are generally served up by hackers and then picked up as news by US Big Media and Social Media. Humiliating as it is for the individuals involved, this nefarious CYBER-vandalism is not a national security matter, but it is used, gleefully, by any number of political interest groups and businesses for their own ends.

In like manner, the Sony, Democratic National Committee and Yahoo electronic break-ins, for example, are not national security incidents by any stretch of the imagination. Were they criminal actions and embarrassing for the victims? Yes. Did the information peddled by the hackers influence the public in some fashion? Sure. If sponsors of the hackers are from Russia, China, Iran, DPRK, Daesh, Israel or any other cyber-suspect, should they be exposed and brought to justice? Yes.

We should not nuke them or carpet-bomb them for such offenses.

It is problematic that politico-military strategists and tacticians, spurred on by any number of think tanks and CYBER hustlers in Washington, DC and New York (Atlantic Council, New York Times), have pushed the robbery of data/information and vandalism, or defacement of main-page websites into a crisis that threatens the nation's stability. More's the pity, they have pasted CYBER over Information Warfare and have meshed it with Asymmetric Warfare and Unconventional Warfare not recognizing the differences and nuances.

CYBER Influence Peddlers: Pest Control Needed

CYBER enthusiasts at the Atlantic Council and the New York Times see foreign news agencies like Xinhua/People's Daily, Press TV, RT, Sputnik News and Hezbollah, which all broadcast news and information with their brand of spin, as demonic CYBER influence peddlers who are corrupting the American national consciousness by engaging in perception management techniques in an attempt to electronically captivate American audiences and turn them, well, to the "dark side."

Iran's Press TV Internet traffic statistics show it is ranked 26,598 with 28 percent of its visits coming from the United States. RT is ranked 446 in the world with 18 percent of its visitors from the US. Sputnik News is 1410 with 8 percent of its visitors from the US. Xinhua is ranked 25,000 with about 3 percent visiting from the US and the People's Daily does not even rank.

In this dark CYBER world, the unemployed and disaffected youth bulges (but why are they jobless and disenchanted), social miscreants and American citizens will populate evil foreign websites and after viewing assorted marketing/propaganda they will by Pepsi instead of Coke; whoops, I meant to say join the Islamic State or the Chinese

151

Communist Party; move to Russia; or take in the Hezbollah
website (huge NBA fans BTW).

What this says, in part, is that those pushing CYBER fear have
unwittingly indicted the United States and its people of idiocy.
They seem to be saying that the American people have been ill
served by the Constitution and the Bill of Rights, educational
institutions and the government and the citizenry is but a
collective of dolts incapable of sorting through information
pushed out of non-Western media outlets. In the United States,
the First Amendment makes sure that all-points of view can be
aired on the premise that the American people have the ability
to harvest information and distinguish between info-crap and
'actionable' info that can be turned into positive knowledge for
civil good.

What is there to fear from comparatively small state backed-
foreign news outlets? So they spin news or publish opinions
contrary to the US narrative. So what? How is that any
different from left and right wing publications in the United
States that take down US civilian and military institutions? The
American public can handle all of this. The CYBER Fear
pushers further display their ignorance by assuming that the US
national security machinery has not done enough to protect the
enfeebled American public from opinions emanating from non-
Western sources. The CYBER chicken-littles believe, too, that
the US military and the chiefs of America's critical
infrastructure sets do not understand the gravity of the CYBER
Danger.

Nonsense!

US MILITARY'S PROGRESSIVENESS
Sleep Well

As the US Army's Unconventional Warfare Manual and scores of US military CYBER commands, and doctrinal publications make clear, the US national security community has been pushing the CYBER matter hard. It has engaged in the less public relations friendly issues like mathematics and encryption, physically securing communications nodes and networks, creating honeypots to attract hackers, digital forensics (breaking into secure hard drives, software) and working with civilian counterparts, sometimes controversially, to secure communications networks.

For those worried about the US government's ability to listen to adversaries, allies, the public, whomever, the Snowden document dumps show just how deep the National Security Agency's wormhole goes. Either you're of the mind that this grossly oversteps the US government's authority, or maybe the nation is better off with the NSA playing God, or, like most, you just don't care.

The US capabilities to tap transoceanic communications cables or satellite communications are well known.

The seriousness with which the US national security community views CYBER can be noted in this comment from a Defense Science Board study on CYBER Existentialism

"While the manifestation of a nuclear and cyber attack are very different, in the end, the existential impact to the United States is the same. Existential Cyber Attack is defined as an attack that is capable of causing sufficient wide scale damage for the government potentially to lose control of the country, including loss or damage to significant portions of military and critical infrastructure: power generation, communications, fuel

and transportation, emergency services, financial services, etch. (Visit the Defense Science Board's website to access the document.)

So a quasi-authoritative US government body claims there is a real danger of an existential CYBER attack. The Atlantic Council and New York Times hyperventilate over Information Warfare. Well, American citizens can take care of themselves and form their own opinions thanks to the First Amendment and access to the WWW.

Whether electronically connected networks collapse because of CYBER Attack, lightning bolts, human error or solar fares, life will go on for those who have the ability to adapt in a crisis.

"Cyber Warfare, Cyber Security and massive Cyber Attacks are alarmist and vastly overrated. Look at what went on in Cyprus in 2013. What could trigger a run on the banks in the United States? Something as simple as shutting down all the ATM's for three days. The resulting panic and long bank lines could irrevocably shake confidence in banks and financial institutions, as Americans find out the significance of all the paperwork they signed when they established their banks accounts, fed by direct deposits. Since many in the country know what the country was like before personal computers and the Internet, they'll do fine. Those people who have exchanged their hearts and brains for computer chips manufactured in Vietnam, and are tethered to Smart Phones and the Cloud, are due for a very rude awakening. You've heard of sleeper agents and moles haven't you? I wonder how many sleeper programs are in the millions of computer chips that are now in every single facet of our lives."